United States
Department of
Agriculture

Forest Service

**Northeastern
Research Station**

General Technical
Report NE-328

ROMI-3: Rough-Mill Simulator Version 3.0: User's Guide

Joel M. Weiss
R. Edward Thomas

Abstract

The ROugh MIll simulator (ROMI Version 3.0) is a computer software package for personal computers that simulates current industrial practices for rip-first and chop-first lumber processing. This guide shows the user how to set up and examine the results of simulations of current or proposed mill practices. ROMI-3 accepts cutting bills with as many as 600 combined solid and/or panel part sizes. Plots of processed boards are easily viewed or printed, as are detailed summaries of processing data (number of rips and crosscuts) and yields for each grade.

The Authors

JOEL M. WEISS is a computer programmer with the Northeastern Research Station's Forestry Sciences Laboratory at Princeton, West Virginia. He received a B.S. degree in computer information systems from Concord College in 2000. He joined the USDA Forest Service in 1999 and currently is engaged in the development of rough-mill simulation and related software systems.

R. EDWARD THOMAS is a research computer scientist with the Northeastern Research Station's Forestry Sciences Laboratory at Princeton, West Virginia. He received a B.S. degree in computer science and philosophy from Concord College in 1988 and an M.S. degree in computer science from West Virginia University in 1993. He joined the USDA Forest Service in 1988 and currently is engaged in the research and development of rough-mill simulation and log and lumber scanning systems.

Contents

1. Introduction 1

2. Installation 3
  2.1 Running the Install Program 3
  2.2 Java Virtual Machine Installation 4
  2.3 ROMI-3.0 Installation 8
  2.4 Starting ROMI-3 11
  2.5 UGRS Installation 13

3. Using ROMI-3 14
  3.1 Defining and Selecting Part Grades 14
    3.1.1 Clear-Two-Face Part Grades 17
    3.1.2 Clear-One-Face Part Grades 17
    3.1.3 Sound-Two-Face Part Grades 19
    3.1.4 Re-rip/Salvage Part Grades 19
    3.1.5 Part Grades: Width Edge Proximity Rules 20
  3.2 Cutting Bill Setup 21
    3.2.1 Opening and Importing Cutting Bills 22
    3.2.2 Cutting Bill Editing 23
    3.2.3 Cutting Modes 24
    3.2.4 Chopsaw Setup 25
    3.2.5 Ripsaw Setup 26
    3.2.6 Mill Control Setup 30
    3.2.7 Salvage Parts Setup 31
    3.2.8 Prioritization Setup 32
    3.2.9 Part Scheduling and Replacement 33

4. Datafile Selection 34
  4.1 Creating Custom Grade Mix and Specified Files 34
    4.1.1 Custom Grade Mix 35
    4.1.2 Choose Boards 38
    4.1.3 File Control 40
  4.2 Data Graph 41

5. Output Options 43
  5.1 Selecting an Output File 44
  5.2 Summary Tables 44
  5.3 Flow Simulation Output 44
  5.4 Length and Width Ranges 45

6. Starting the Analysis 46
   6.1 Interactive Mode 47
   6.2 Batch Mode 47
7. Simulation Results 49
   7.1 Yield Summary Results 50
   7.2 Summary Table Results 50
   7.3 Cutting Bill Results 51
   7.4 Board Plots 52

8. Least Cost Grade Mix 54
   8.1 Least Cost Grade Mix Setup 55
   8.2 Least Cost Grade Mix Results 55

9. The Mechanics of ROMI-3 57
   9.1. Gang-Ripsaws 57
      9.1.1. Fixed Blade Arbors 57
      9.1.2. Best-Spacing-Sequence Arbors 59
      9.1.3. All-Blades-Movable Arbor 60
      9.1.4. Optimizing Arbor Comparison 60
      9.1.5. How to Optimize Fixed-Blade Saw Spacing Sequences 63
   9.2. Part Prioritization 63
      9.2.1. Value-Based Part Prioritizing 64
      9.2.2. Area-Based Part Prioritizing 64
      9.2.3 Dynamic Part Prioritizing 65
      9.2.4 Selecting a Part-Prioritizing Strategy 66
   9.3. Processing Salvage Parts 66
      9.3.1. Locating Clear Salvage Areas 66
      9.3.2. Selecting a Clear Area 67
      9.3.3. Producing the Salvage Part 67
      9.3.4. Smart Salvage 68

Literature Cited 70

Appendix I. System Limitations 72
Appendix II. Board Data Bank Description 73
Appendix III. Definition of Terms 74

1. Introduction

Version 3.0 of the ROMI (ROugh MIll Simulator) is the latest in a series of rough-mill simulation programs developed by the USDA Forest Service. The ROMI-3 install CD contains sample runs, all required programs, and the "1998 Data Bank for Kiln-Dried Red Oak Lumber" (Gatchell et al. 1998), which includes more than 3,000 digitized boards. A digitized board is a real board whose dimensions and defects are expressed in x,y coordinates. An included custom datafile creation utility allows you to create board samples corresponding to your lumber supply. ROMI-3 processes the board data according to your processing specifications. Output, including part counts and yields, graphical plots of processed boards, and processing requirements are available from each run. This guide shows you how to install and run ROMI-3 as well as design simulations to answer questions related to rough-mill processing.

The ROMI-3 simulator incorporates both rip-first and chop-first processing into a single program. As such, ROMI-3 officially replaces the ROMI-RIP 2.0 (Thomas 1999) and ROMI-CROSS (Thomas 1997) computer programs. ROMI-3 can import all settings and cutting bills from the earlier simulators. Like ROMI-RIP and ROMI-CROSS, ROMI-3 can produce parts of different grade or quality specifications to simulate the production of clear-two-face (C2F), clear-one-face (C1F), and sound-two-face (S2F) parts. ROMI-3 supports part scheduling and replacement and allows the user to define the maximum number of part sizes to process at once, as well as replace part sizes as requirements are met. This latest version also supports the production of solids, panels or glue-up, and random-length parts. For our purposes, a panel or glue-up part is made of two or more solid parts that have been edge-glued together.

New features of ROMI-3 include an optimum arbor generation tool and a least-cost-grade-mix calculator. The arbor generation tool determines the optimum fixed-blade saw-spacing-sequence for a specific cutting bill and lumber-size distribution. The least-cost-grade-mix calculator determines the most cost-efficient grade mix for a specific cutting bill with respect to both lumber and processing costs. A new fixed-blade-best-feed arbor type optimizes for the production of strips much like a good ripsaw operator would, resulting in more realistic simulation results.

The minimum computer system requirements to run ROMI-3 are:

- An Apple Power Macintosh with a 300 MHz G3 CPU or newer[1]
- An IBM Compatible PC with a 400 MHz Pentium® II or newer[1]
- 64 MB of RAM
- 200 MB hard drive space available
- Linux, Apple OS X, or Microsoft Windows 95/98/ME/2000/XP[1]
- CD-ROM
- Printer (optional but recommended)
- Internet connection (optional but recommended)

To avoid confusion and make this user's guide easier to understand, several conventions have been adopted for displaying operating system and ROMI-3 prompts and input. For all prompts and buttons, Helvetica Italicized is used; for all user input, Helvetica Bold is used.

---

[1]The use of trade, firm, or corporation names in this publication is for the information and convenience of the reader. Such use does not constitute an official endorsement or approval by the U.S. Department of Agriculture or the Forest Service of any product or service to the exclusion of others that may be suitable. Power Macintosh and OSX are a registered trademark of Apple Computer, Inc., Linux is a registered trademark of Linus Torvalds, Windows 95, 98, ME, 2000, and XP are registered trademarks of Microsoft Corporation, Inc., Pentium® is a registered trademark of Intel Corporation.

2. Installation

2.1 Running the Install Program

To install, place the ROMI-3 CD into the CD-ROM drive of your computer. If the auto run feature is enabled, it will automatically start the setup procedure and bring up the window in Figure 2.1a.

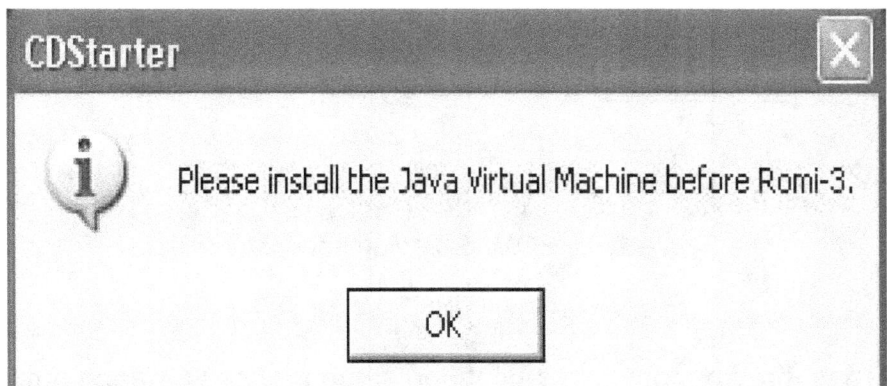

Figure 2.1a. Auto run window.

If the box in Figure 2.1a. is not displayed, click *start* and then *run*. In the run window, type "**d:\install**" without the quotes, substituting the letter d for the appropriate letter of your CD-ROM drive, and click *OK*. You should see the window in Figure 2.1a, which informs you that the Java Virtual Machine[2] (JVM) must be installed before you install ROMI-3. Click *OK* to bring up the window in Figure 2.1b.

---

[2]Java Virtual Machine (JVM) is a registered trademark of Sun Microsystems, Inc.

Figure 2.1b. ROMI-3.0 setup and install window.

This window has three buttons that launch the setup routines for each program. The first one is the *Java Virtual Machine* that is used by ROMI-3 and **must be installed**. If you have previously installed the *Java Virtual Machine*, proceed to the installation of ROMI-3 or UGRS.

2.2 Java Virtual Machine Installation

When the Java Virtual Machine button is clicked, you will see the screen in Figure 2.2a.

4

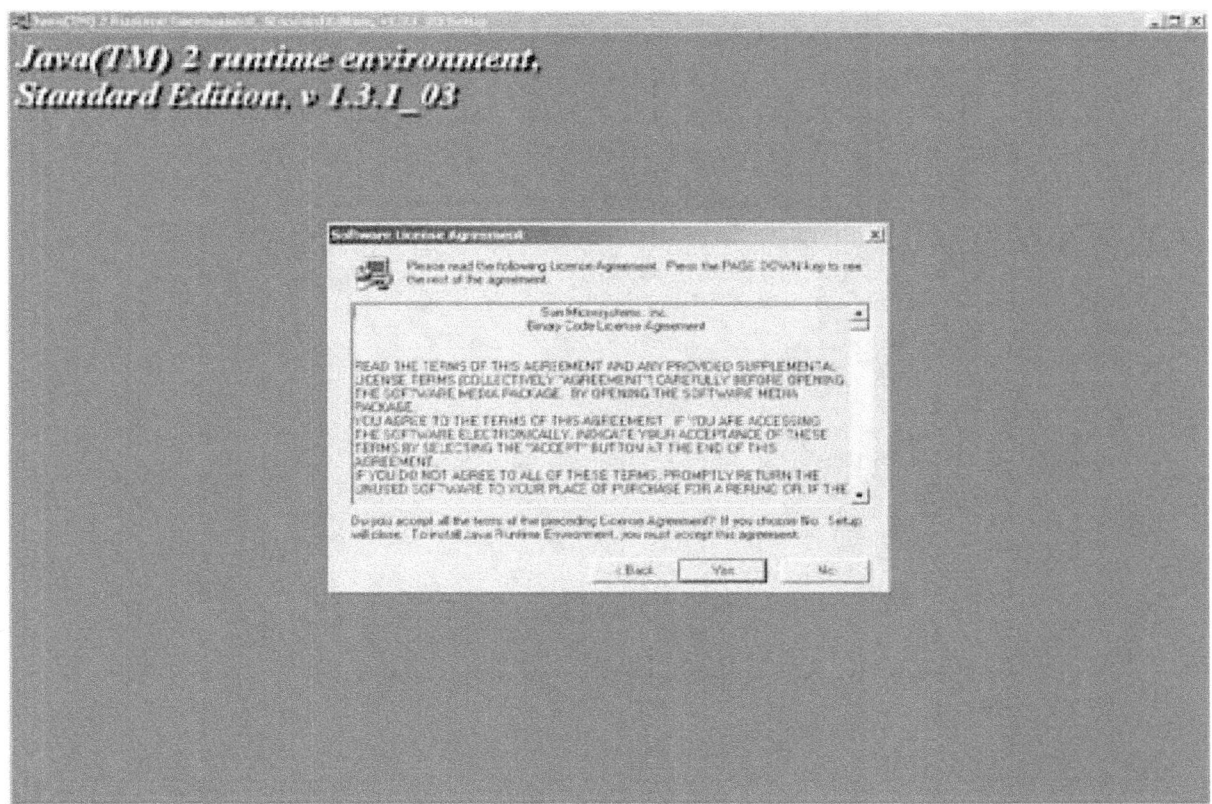

Figure 2.2a. Java Runtime Environment (JRE) install screen.

This is the license agreement for Sun Microsystems software that you must accept before you can continue. Click yes to bring up the next screen (Fig. 2.2b.), which displays the directory in which the *Java Virtual Machine* will be installed.

5

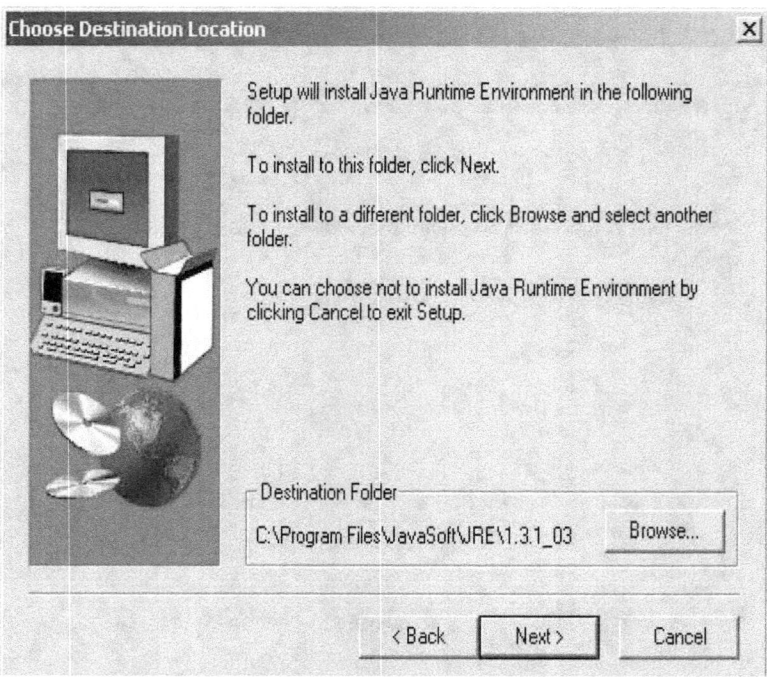

Figure 2.2b. Java Runtime Environment destination window.

You can choose the default directory or click *browse* to change it. Click *next* to bring up the screen in Figure 2.2c.

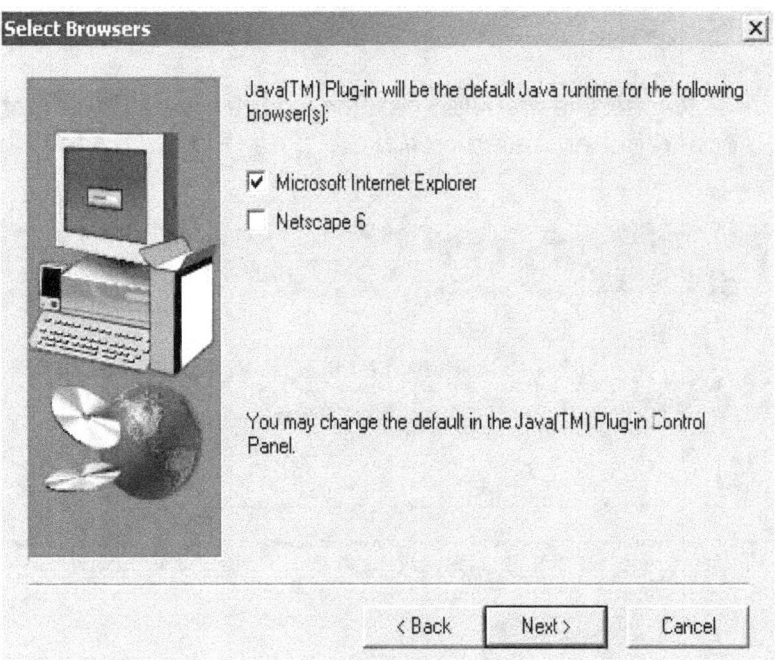

Figure 2.2c. Window to choose browser to use with Java runtime.

This screen lists the internet browsers installed on your machine. You can uncheck all of the boxes as this does not affect ROMI-3. Click *next* to start the installation. Depending on your version of Windows, you may be asked to restart your machine. If you have to reboot, you must start the main install procedure again by following the steps outlined in section 1.1. If not, the screen in Figure 2.1b. will be shown again.

2.3 ROMI-3.0 Installation

Once the *Java Virtual Machine* is installed, you can continue with the installation of ROMI-3. Click the second button called *ROMI-3.0 beta* (Fig. 2.1b.) to bring up the screen in Figure 2.3a.

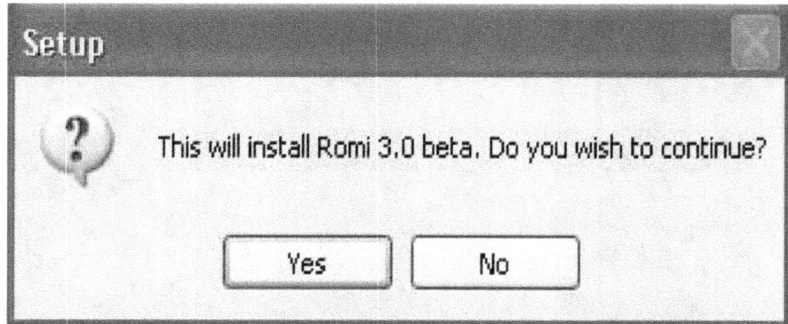

Figure 2.3a. ROMI-3.0 beta install confirmation window.

Click *yes* to start the ROMI-3 setup wizard. You should see the welcome screen in Figure 2.3b.

Figure 2.3b. ROMI-3.0 beta Setup Wizard window.

Click *next* to see the default install directory and a directory listing of the files on your computer (Fig. 2.3c.).

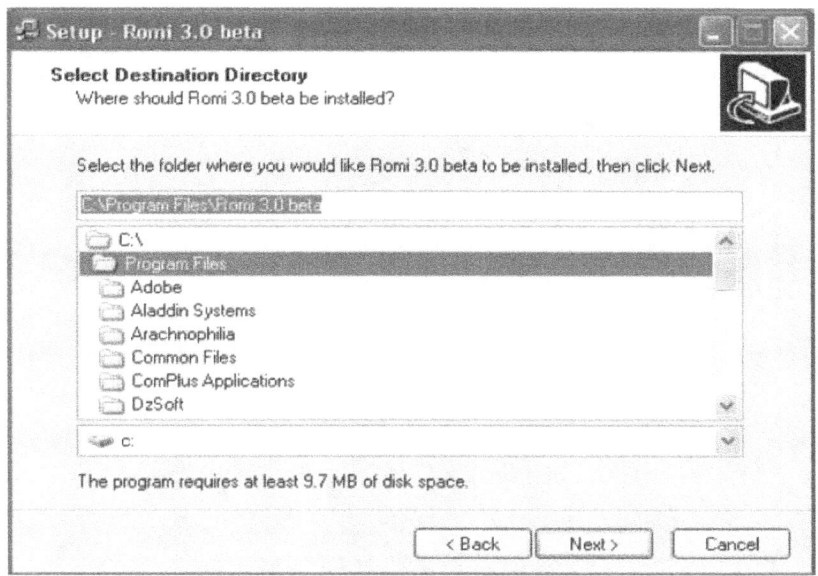

Figure 2.3c. ROMI-3.0 beta destination window.

If you want to keep the default install directory, click *next*. If you want to change it, you can browse the directories by double-clicking the file names or by manually entering a path in the box at the top of the window. To change the drive you are browsing, click the *drop down arrow* at the bottom right of the screen. Click *next* when you are satisfied with the install directory. You will see the screen in Figure 2.3d.

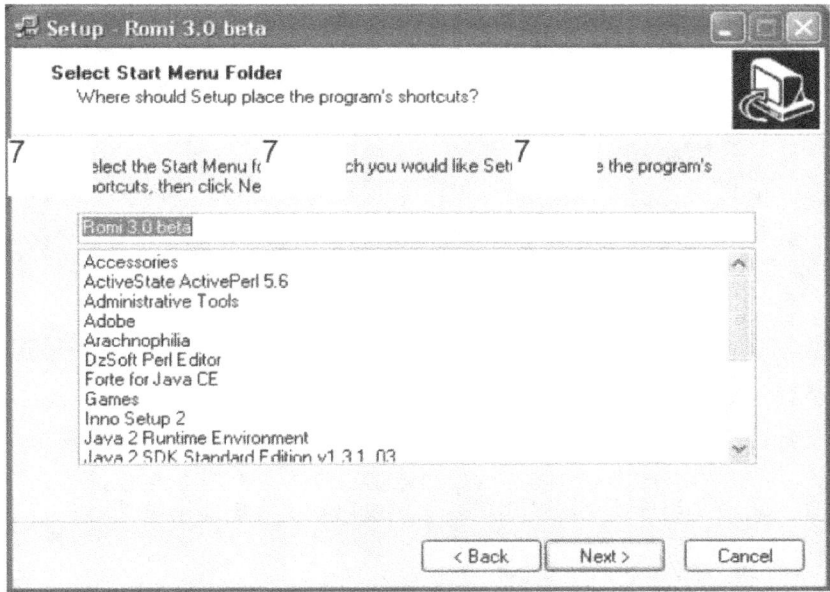

Figure 2.3d. Start Menu folder window.

On this screen you can change the name that will be displayed in the start menu. Click *next* if you are satisfied with the default name; otherwise, you can change it and click *next* to bring up the screen in Figure 2.3e.

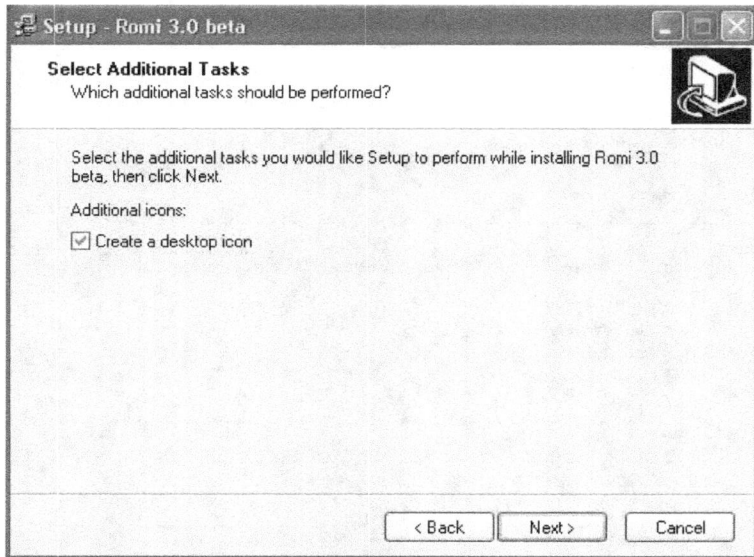

Figure 2.3e. Create desktop icon window.

If you want the install procedure to place a shortcut icon on your desktop, leave the check in the box and click *next*. If you do not want an icon, remove it and click *next*. You are now ready to install ROMI-3. The window (Fig. 2.3f.) now shows the setup options you have selected.

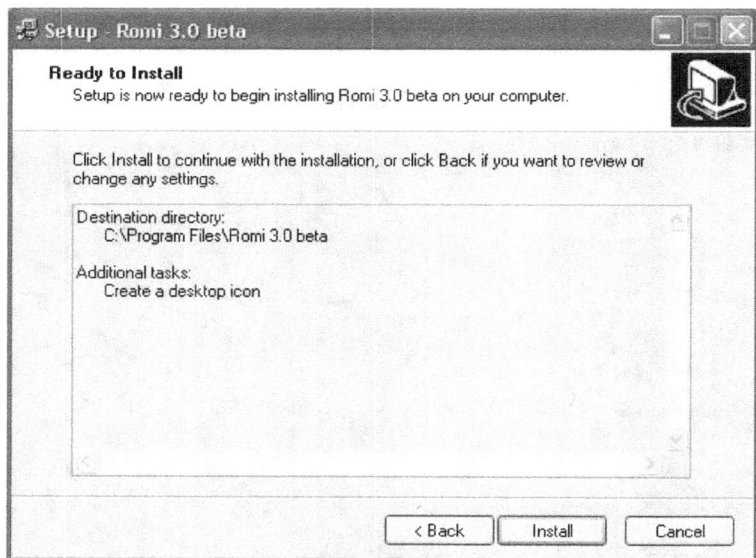

Figure 2.3f. ROMI-3.0 beta settings confirmation window.

Make sure the install options are correct and click *install*. The installation may take some time depending on the speed of your computer. When it is finished, you will see the last screen (Fig. 2.3g.) of the installation.

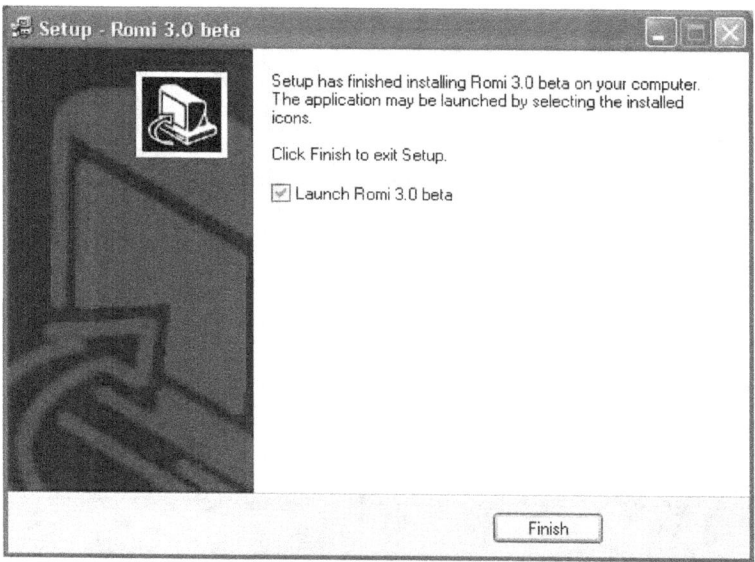

Figure 2.3g. Install finished window.

If you want to start ROMI-3 immediately, leave the check in the box and click *finish*. If you want to wait before starting ROMI-3, make sure the check box is clear and click *finish*.

2.4 Starting ROMI-3

There are two ways to start ROMI-3. If you chose to create a desktop icon (Fig. 2.3e.), double-click the desktop icon *ROMI-3.0 beta* to bring up the main interface (Fig. 2.4a.). Or clicking *start* and then *programs* (All Programs in Windows XP) will display the name you chose in the step described by Figure 2.3d. If you kept the default name, it will be ROMI-3.0 beta. You should see an arrow out from the name indicating there is a submenu. Move the mouse over the name and the menu will show four items. The first is Register for Updates that will take you to a simple form on the Internet. If you have an Internet connection and wish to be notified when an update is available, click this and fill out the form. The second item is ROMI-3.0 beta. Clicking this will start the main program and you should see the main window (Fig. 2.4a.).

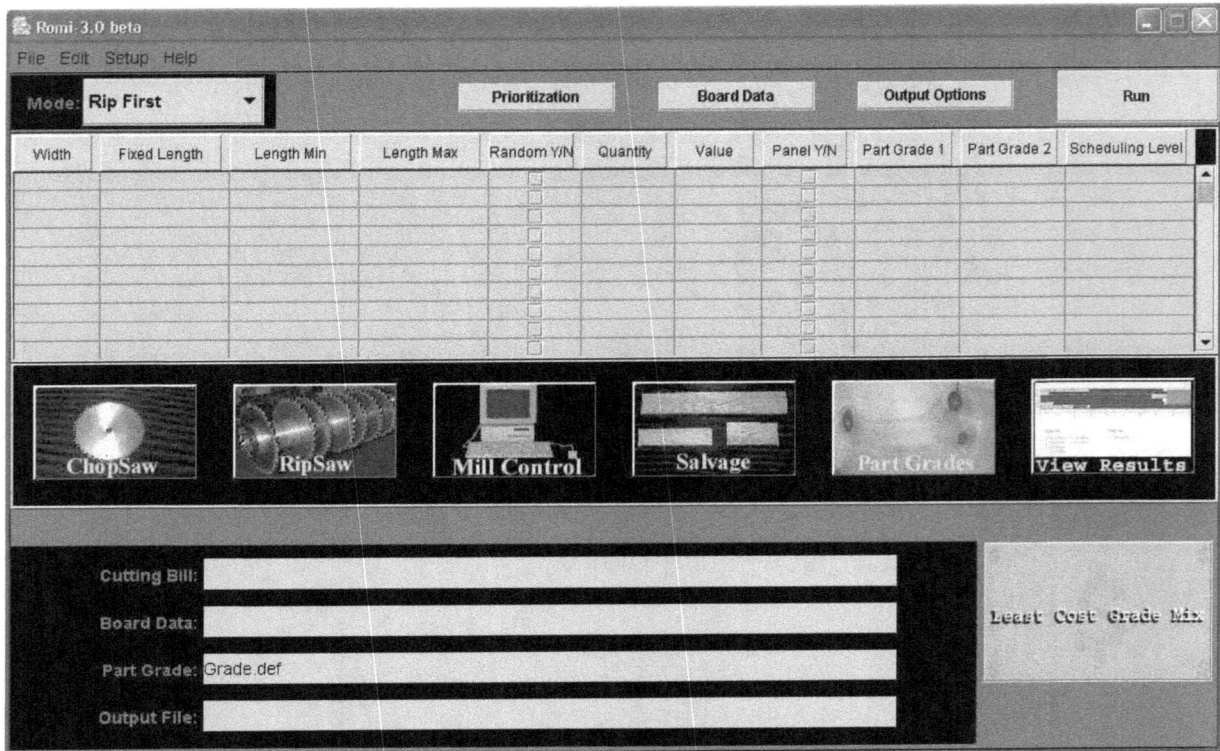

Figure 2.4a. Main ROMI-3 interface window.

The third item is a link to the main ROMI-3 webpage. If you are notified that there is an update, this is where you would go to download the latest version of ROMI-3. The last item in the list is Uninstall ROMI-3.0 beta that can be used to uninstall ROMI-3.

2.5 UGRS Installation

The Ultimate Grading and Remanufacturing System (UGRS) (Moody et al. 1998) is a computer program designed to help the user better understand the National Hardwood Lumber Association's (NHLA) lumber grading system (NHLA 1998). The UGRS program interactively trains the user, grades lumber, and can remanufacture lumber for maximum dollar value. The user-interface presents both faces of the board to the user as well as all defects and cuttings, grading information, the remanufactured board, and final results. UGRS operates only under the Microsoft Windows operating systems.

The UGRS installation is optional as it is not used or required by the ROMI-3 simulator. However, you may find UGRS to be a useful education tool. If you are not interested in UGRS, click **close** on the main installation screen and skip to section 3 of this manual. To install UGRS, click "**UGRS**" on the main installation window (Fig. 2.1b.). You will see the window in Figure 2.5a. To complete the installation, follow the steps used to install ROMI-3.0.

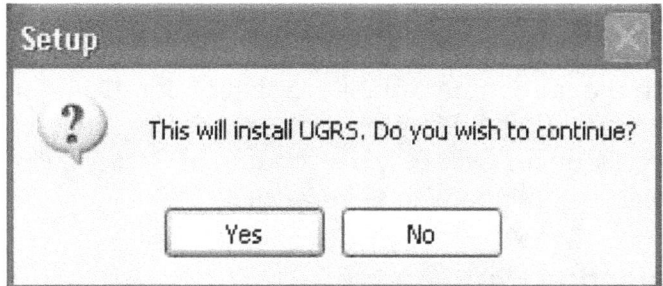

Figure 2.5a. UGRS install confirmation window.

3. Using ROMI-3

It is important that the steps for a ROMI-3 simulation be performed in the correct order. For example, part qualities must be defined before specifying cutting bill parts. You also need to define your cutting bill before setting up the arbor. However, if you need only minor changes, the order in which you perform them is less important. This section leads you through all these steps by showing you how to set up an analysis for a sample cutting bill. To become familiar with ROMI- 3, you may want to work along with the example. In any case, the basic sequence of steps in setting up any ROMI-3 analysis is:

1) Select or define a part-quality definition file
2) Enter the cutting bill part sizes and quantities
3) Set up the arbor and chopsaws
4) Set up the overall processing and control options
5) Specify the salvage part sizes (if any)
6) Define output options
7) Select board data to process
8) Run and analyze simulation results

Some steps need to be taken only once despite the number of simulations that are run. For example, if you use a common part quality definition for all cutting bills, enter it only once and use it for each run. If you use the same processing options for every cutting bill, you need define them only once. One of the strengths of ROMI-3 is that you can examine many alternative processing options with several clicks.

3.1 Defining and Selecting Part Grades

A powerful feature of ROMI-3 is the ability to process multiple part grades. ROMI-3 allows the user to specify a range of defect types, sizes, acceptable distances from part edge, and whether each defect is acceptable on the face, back, or both faces. Users can define as many different part grades as required. In the absence of low grade material, a higher grade is substituted automatically. This does not waste high-quality part areas in low-quality parts. This is accomplished by optimizing for the highest quality parts in the first pass, the next highest quality in the second pass, and so on. During each pass, the parts with the highest priority and part quality are marked for removal. Any remaining area is downgraded according to adjacent quality areas. For example, an area too short for any part with a quality of 1 adjacent to an area with a quality of 3 would be downgraded to quality 3. In the absence of adjacent areas with a lower part quality, the entire area is downgraded to the next available quality. A strip is processed by the chopsaw when parts have been placed in all usable quality areas.

A part grade consists of one or more rules. Each rule specifies that a defect or category of defects is acceptable on a single part face. To open the part grades editor, click *Part Grades* in the main ROMI-3 interface (Fig. 2.4a.). You will see a window displaying the current part grade information (Fig. 3.1a.).

File

Grade Code	Side	Defect Code	Description	Proximity	min Proximity	max Proximity	Re-Rip
0	Face	0	Scrap, All Defects	☐	0.0000	0.0000	☐
1	Face	999	Clear, No Defect	☐	0.0000	0.0000	☐
2	Face	999	Clear, No Defect	☐	0.0	0.0	☑
5	Face	4	Decay	☐	0.5	1.25	☐
5	Face	4	Decay	☐	0.5	1.25	☐
5	Face	9	Sawline	☐	0.5	1.25	☐
5	Face	9	Sawline	☐	0.5	1.25	☐
6	Face	1	Mechanical damage	☑	0.125	10	☐
6	Face	1	Mechanical damage	☑	0.125	10	☐
6	Face	12	All unsound knots	☑	0.75	10	☐
6	Face	12	All unsound knots	☑	0.75	10	☐
7	Face	1	Mechanical damage	☑	0.5	1.0	☐
7	Face	1	Mechanical damage	☑	0.5	1.0	☐
7	Face	2	Void	☑	0.5	1.0	☐
7	Face	3	Pith	☑	0.5	1.0	☐

Figure 3.1a. Part Grade Editor window showing default part grade file.

By default, the file named Grade.def is loaded into the part grade editor. Grade definition files from ROMI-2 also can be used in ROMI-3. To use a saved definition file, click *File* and then *Open*. You will see a file open window (Fig. 3.1b.).

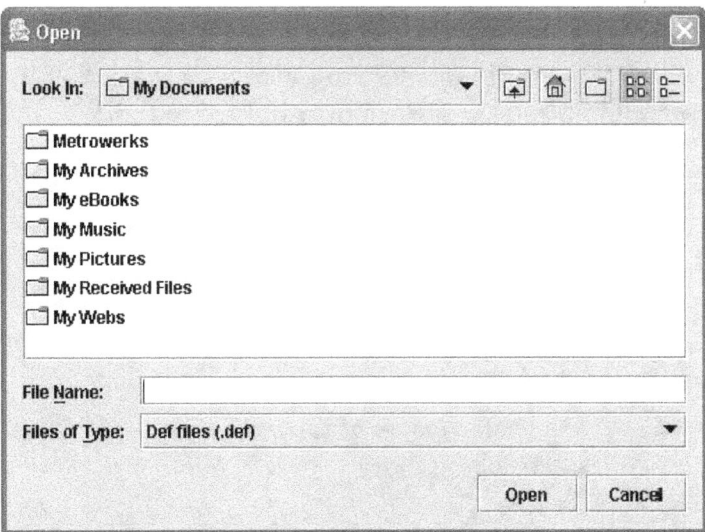

Figure 3.1b. Part Grade Definition file chooser.

Navigate to the file you want and double-click the file name to open it. Your definition file will be displayed in the part grade editor.

To define a set of custom part grades, you can start a blank file or edit an existing file. To start a new part grade file, click *File* and then *New* to clear everything but the first two rows. The first two rows, scrap and clear-two-face (C2F), are mandatory and cannot be changed. ROMI-3 uses scrap internally to identify all board areas that do not meet any part grade definition, so no parts can be cut from scrap. A part grade specification file is composed of one or more part grades, which, in turn, are composed of one or more rules. The rules for a single grade have the same grade code (Fig 3.1a). Grade codes are sorted so that all of the rules of a single grade are listed together. There are several kinds of information that must be specified for a part grade specification file (This information is covered in detail in this section). Starting at the third row, double-click in the Grade Code, Min Proximity, or the Max Proximity columns to bring up the window in Figure 3.1c.

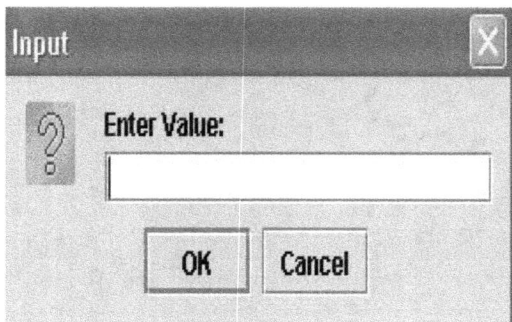

Figure 3.1c. Input dialog box.

Enter the desired value into the text box and click *OK*. The second column indicates the Side of the board to allow the defined defect to be on. Values can be toggled from Face to Back by double-clicking in the cell you want to change. The third and fourth columns are Defect Codes and Description. Each defect code has a description so if you change the value in one, the corresponding code or description will be placed in the other. To change these, double-click the cell to bring up the window in Figure 3.1d.

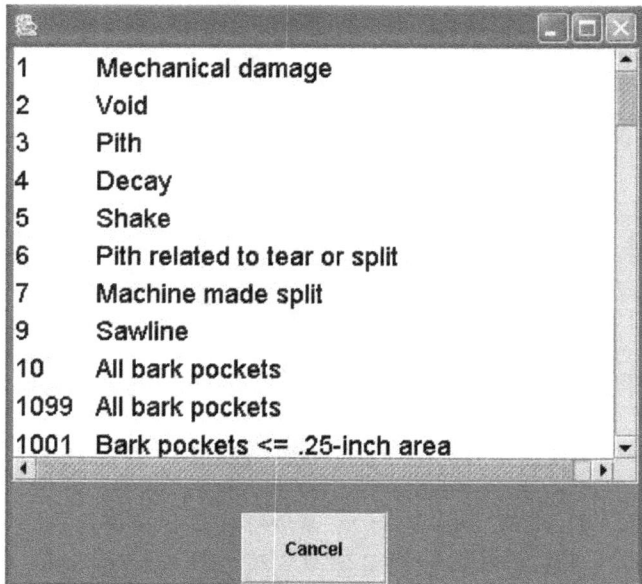

Figure 3.1d. Defect chooser window.

16

Use the scroll bar to view all of the available defects and click the one you want. Column five is Proximity and column eight is Re-Rip. Both contain check boxes (a check means yes and the absence of a check means no). You can click the box with the mouse or move to the cell and use the space bar to toggle on or off. To delete a grade, click on the one you want to delete. The entire row will be highlighted. Clicking *Edit* and then *Delete* will update the table.

3.1.1 Clear-Two-Face Part Grades

Before starting, we will clear the table by clicking *File* and then *New*. All rows except for the first two will be cleared (Fig. 3.1.1a.). Because the second row is a C2F, one of the mandatory grades in a definition file, no entry is necessary.

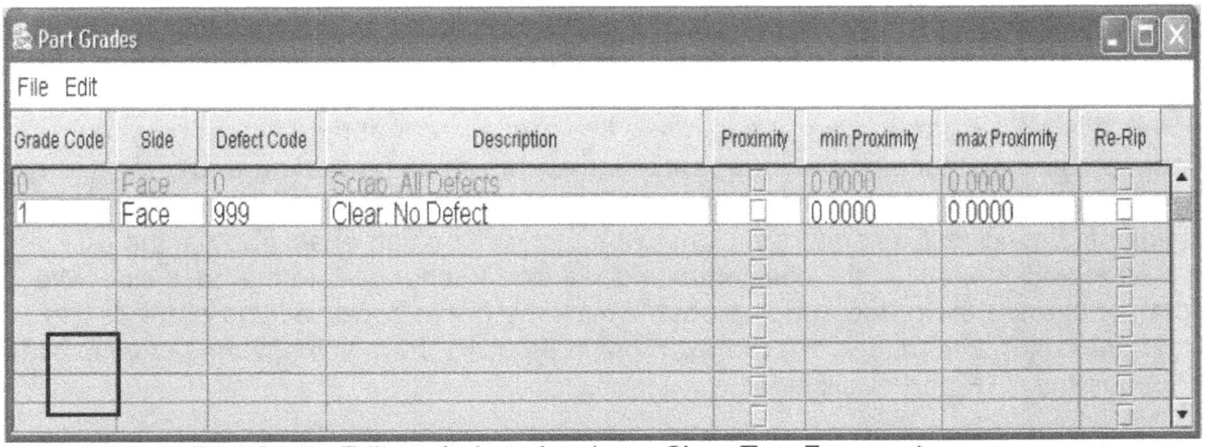

Grade Code	Side	Defect Code	Description	Proximity	min Proximity	max Proximity	Re-Rip
0	Face	0	Scrap. All Defects	☐	0.0000	0.0000	☐
1	Face	999	Clear. No Defect	☐	0.0000	0.0000	☐
				☐			☐
				☐			☐
				☐			☐
				☐			☐
				☐			☐
				☐			☐

Figure 3.1.1a. Part Grade Editor window showing a Clear-Two-Face part.

3.1.2 Clear-One-Face Part Grades

To create a C1F part grade, we must define it as two separate grades: once with defects located on the face and once with defects located on the back. For example, you want a C1F with sound knots less than 1/2 in. surface area. To add this grade, double-click in the first blank cell in the Grade Code column. The next available grade code will be added. Looking at Figure 3.1.1a., if you click the blank cell below the grade code 1, a 2 will be added as the next grade code. To change this code, double-click on it and enter the number you want. Then double-click in the Side column and the value will become **Face**. Now double-click in the Defect Code column. You should see the window in Figure 3.1d. Scroll down the list until you find the sound knot defects and select **sound knots <= .50-inch area**. The defect code and corresponding description will be added to the table. We do not want proximity enabled, so the Proximity columns are ignored. We also leave Re-Rip as is. The table should look like Figure 3.1.2a.

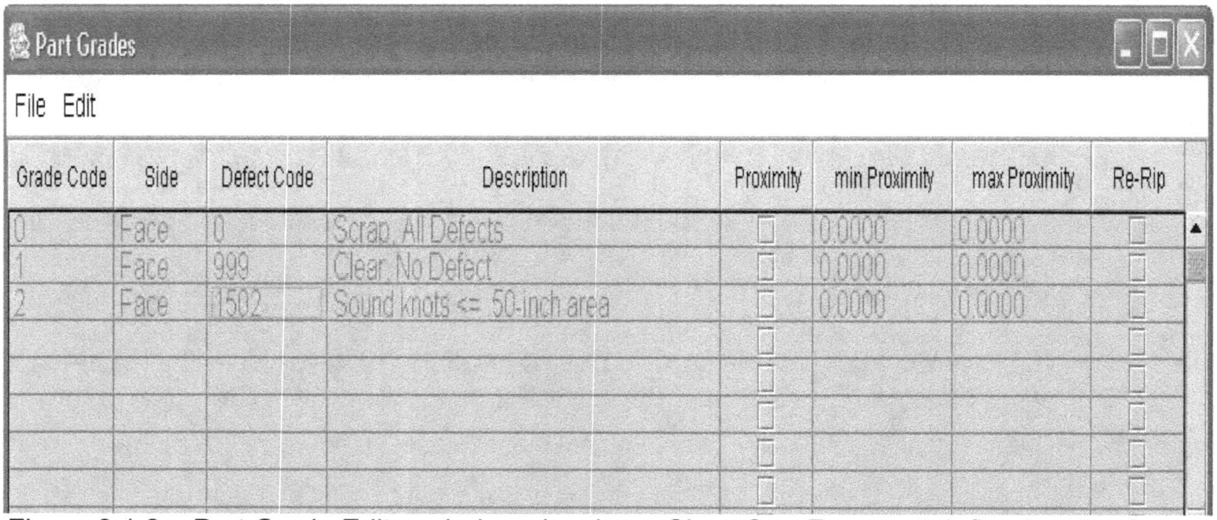

Grade Code	Side	Defect Code	Description	Proximity	min Proximity	max Proximity	Re-Rip
0	Face	0	Scrap, All Defects	☐	0.0000	0.0000	☐
1	Face	999	Clear, No Defect	☐	0.0000	0.0000	☐
2	Face	1502	Sound knots <= 50-inch area	☐	0.0000	0.0000	☐
				☐			☐
				☐			☐
				☐			☐
				☐			☐
				☐			☐

Figure 3.1.2a. Part Grade Editor window showing a Clear-One-Face part defined on the face of a board.

Since this is a C1F grade, we need to make two grades so that the second one has defects on the back face. You can repeat the previous steps for adding a rule and change the side or there is a shortcut for adding rules. First click the rule you want to duplicate to highlight it. Now click *Edit* and then *Copy Rule*. You will see an exact copy of the rule in the next row. Double-click the cell containing the side to change it to the back side. We also must change the grade code so double click the grade code cell and enter 3. The part grade editor should look like the example in Figure 3.1.2b. We now have two grades that define the C1F part quality.

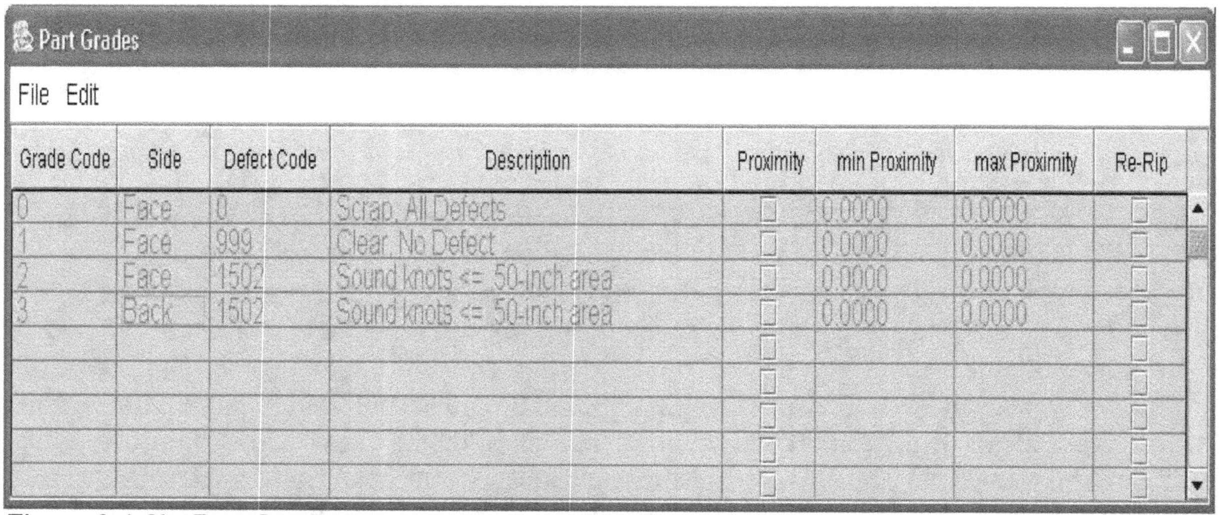

Grade Code	Side	Defect Code	Description	Proximity	min Proximity	max Proximity	Re-Rip
0	Face	0	Scrap, All Defects	☐	0.0000	0.0000	☐
1	Face	999	Clear, No Defect	☐	0.0000	0.0000	☐
2	Face	1502	Sound knots <= 50-inch area	☐	0.0000	0.0000	☐
3	Back	1502	Sound knots <= 50-inch area	☐	0.0000	0.0000	☐
				☐			☐
				☐			☐
				☐			☐
				☐			☐

Figure 3.1.2b. Part Grade Editor window showing a Clear-One-Face part defined on the back of a board.

3.1.3 Sound-Two-Face Part Grades

In most cases, Sound-Two-Face (S2F) part qualities are easier to define than C1F part qualities as only one grade must be defined. For example, you want a S2F grade that defines three defects on each side. First double-click the next blank grade code cell and the next available code will be added. Then double-click the side to add Face. Now double-click the defect code cell and choose defect code **111 Shot worm hole (1/16-1/4) area** from the list. Since we want this rule for both sides, we click the row to highlight it and click *Edit* and then *Copy Rule*. Double-click the side to change it from **Face** to **Back**. Now copy the rule and change the side to Face and change the defect code to a **211 Pin worm hole (< 1/16) area**. Copy this rule and change the side to **Back**. Finally we want defect code **1504 Sound knots <= 1.0-inch area** on both the face and back. When finished, your editor should look like Figure 3.1.3a.

Grade Code	Side	Defect Code	Description	Proximity	min Proximity	max Proximity	Re-Rip
0	Face	0	Scrap, All Defects	☐	0.0000	0.0000	☐
1	Face	999	Clear, No Defect	☐	0.0000	0.0000	☐
2	Face	1502	Sound knots <= 50-inch area	☐	0.0000	0.0000	☐
3	Back	1502	Sound knots <= 50-inch area	☐	0.0000	0.0000	☐
4	Face	111	Shot worm hole (1/16-1/4)" area	☐	0.0000	0.0000	☐
4	Back	111	Shot worm hole (1/16-1/4)" area	☐	0.0000	0.0000	☐
4	Face	211	Pin worm hole (< 1/16)" area	☐	0.0000	0.0000	☐
4	Back	211	Pin worm hole (< 1/16)" area	☐	0.0000	0.0000	☐
4	Face	1504	Sound knots <= 1.0-inch area	☐	0.0000	0.0000	☐
4	Back	1504	Sound knots <= 1.0-inch area	☐	0.0000	0.0000	☐
				☐			☐

Figure 3.1.3a. Part Grade Editor window showing a Sound-Two-Face part.

3.1.4 Re-rip/Salvage Part Grades

The last grade we will define will be a re-rip or salvage part grade. If we want our salvage parts to be C2F, we double-click the next empty grade code cell. A 5 appears as the next available code. Since this is a S2F, we define our defects on the face or back side, but not both. Double-click the cell in the side column to make it **Face**. Then double-click the defect code cell and choose defect code **999 Clear, No Defect**. Since we want this to be a re-rip, double-click the box in the last column under the heading Re-Rip. A checkmark will appear in the box. The completed part grade definition for all our grades should look like Figure 3.1.4a.

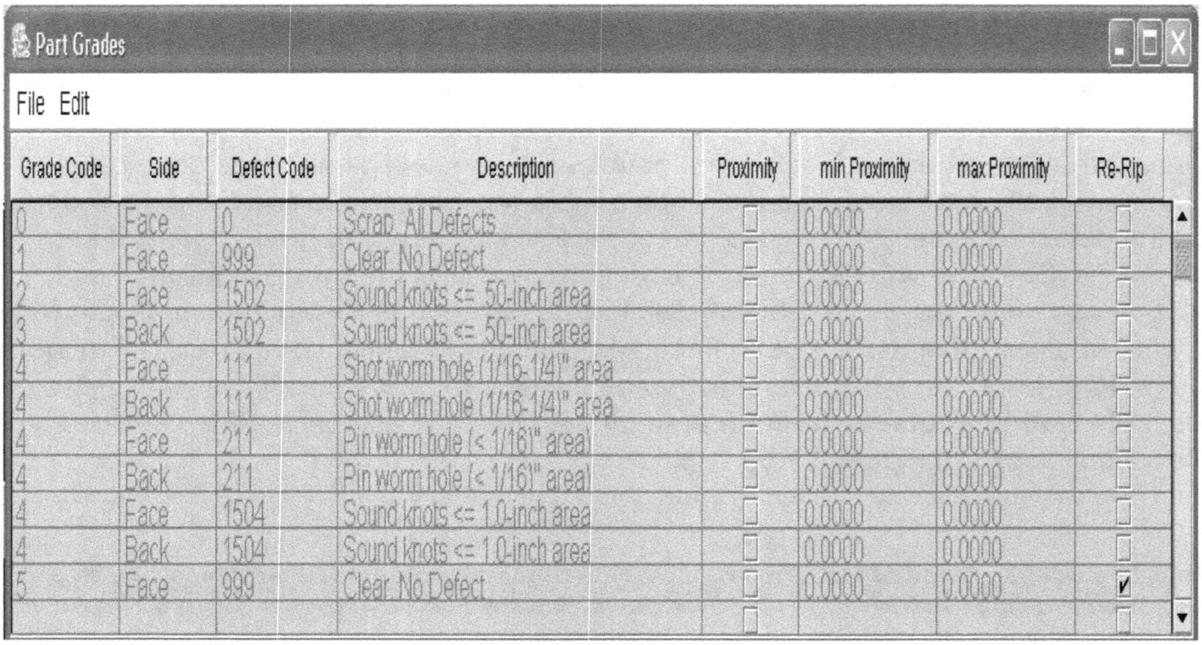

Grade Code	Side	Defect Code	Description	Proximity	min Proximity	max Proximity	Re-Rip
0	Face	0	Scrap. All Defects	☐	0.0000	0.0000	☐
1	Face	999	Clear. No Defect	☐	0.0000	0.0000	☐
2	Face	1502	Sound knots <= 50-inch area	☐	0.0000	0.0000	☐
3	Back	1502	Sound knots <= 50-inch area	☐	0.0000	0.0000	☐
4	Face	111	Shot worm hole (1/16-1/4)" area	☐	0.0000	0.0000	☐
4	Back	111	Shot worm hole (1/16-1/4)" area	☐	0.0000	0.0000	☐
4	Face	211	Pin worm hole (< 1/16)" area	☐	0.0000	0.0000	☐
4	Back	211	Pin worm hole (< 1/16)" area	☐	0.0000	0.0000	☐
4	Face	1504	Sound knots <= 1.0-inch area	☐	0.0000	0.0000	☐
4	Back	1504	Sound knots <= 1.0-inch area	☐	0.0000	0.0000	☐
5	Face	999	Clear. No Defect	☐	0.0000	0.0000	☑
				☐			☐

Figure 3.1.4a. Part Grade Editor window showing a salvage part grade.

Now all that we need to do is save the file. Click *File* and then *Save*. Choose a name for the file and click *OK*.

3.1.5 Part Grades: Width Edge Proximity Rules

A feature not used in the previous examples allows you to define defect types that are acceptable at a specific distance from the edge. This is useful for moulding and millwork parts where defects are acceptable so long as they are not in an area that will be machined. To enable this feature in part grades, double-click the proximity check box in the row of the desired rule. Then double-click the min Proximity cell and enter the minimum acceptable distance from the edge, the same for max Proximity. The result should look like Figure 3.1.5a.

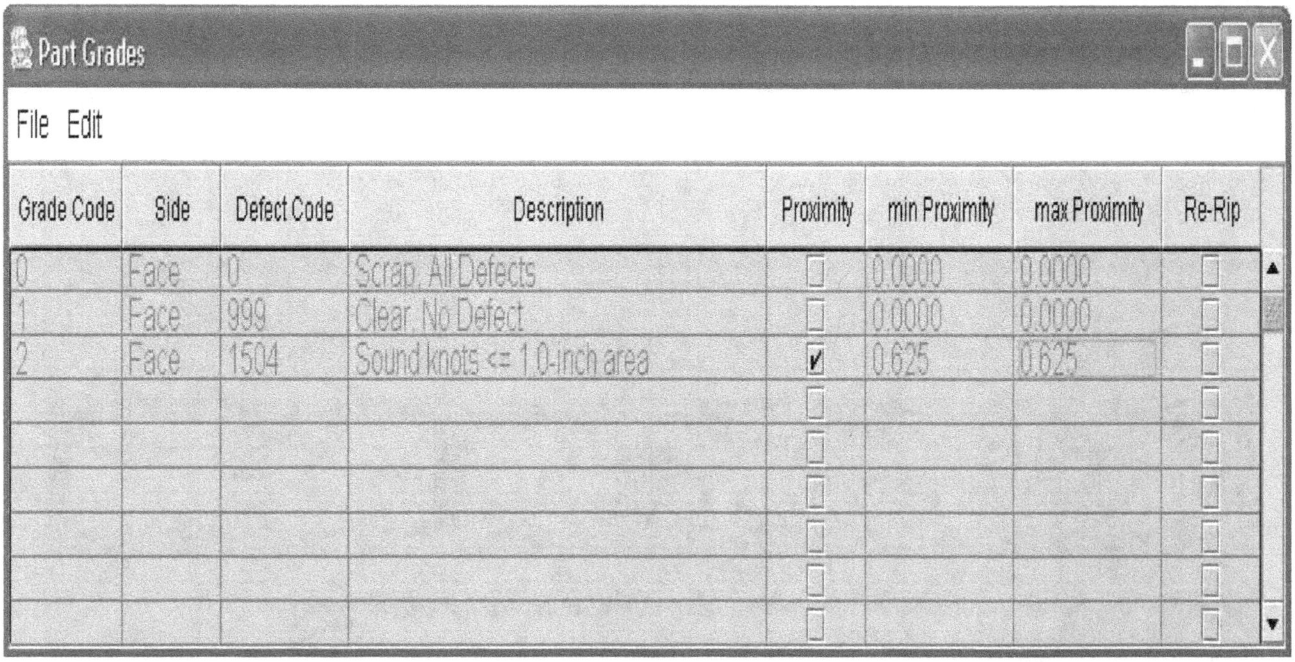

Part Grades

File   Edit

Grade Code	Side	Defect Code	Description	Proximity	min Proximity	max Proximity	Re-Rip
0	Face	0	Scrap, All Defects	☐	0.0000	0.0000	☐
1	Face	999	Clear, No Defect	☐	0.0000	0.0000	☐
2	Face	1504	Sound knots <= 1.0-inch area	☑	0.625	0.625	☐
				☐			☐
				☐			☐
				☐			☐
				☐			☐
				☐			☐
				☐			☐
				☐			☐

Figure 3.1.5a. Part Grade Editor window showing the use of min and max proximity.

If there is no maximum acceptable distance, enter the maximum strip width on which it will be used.

3.2 Cutting Bill Setup

Once part grades have been defined and saved or a part grade file has been selected, you are ready to begin working with the cutting bill. The cutting bill is the central part of the simulation as it defines the part sizes in the numbers and qualities that are required. As such, it ties together the part grade definitions with the individual part requirements and dictates arbor setup as well as other processing options. Figure 3.2a. shows the main interface of ROMI-3.

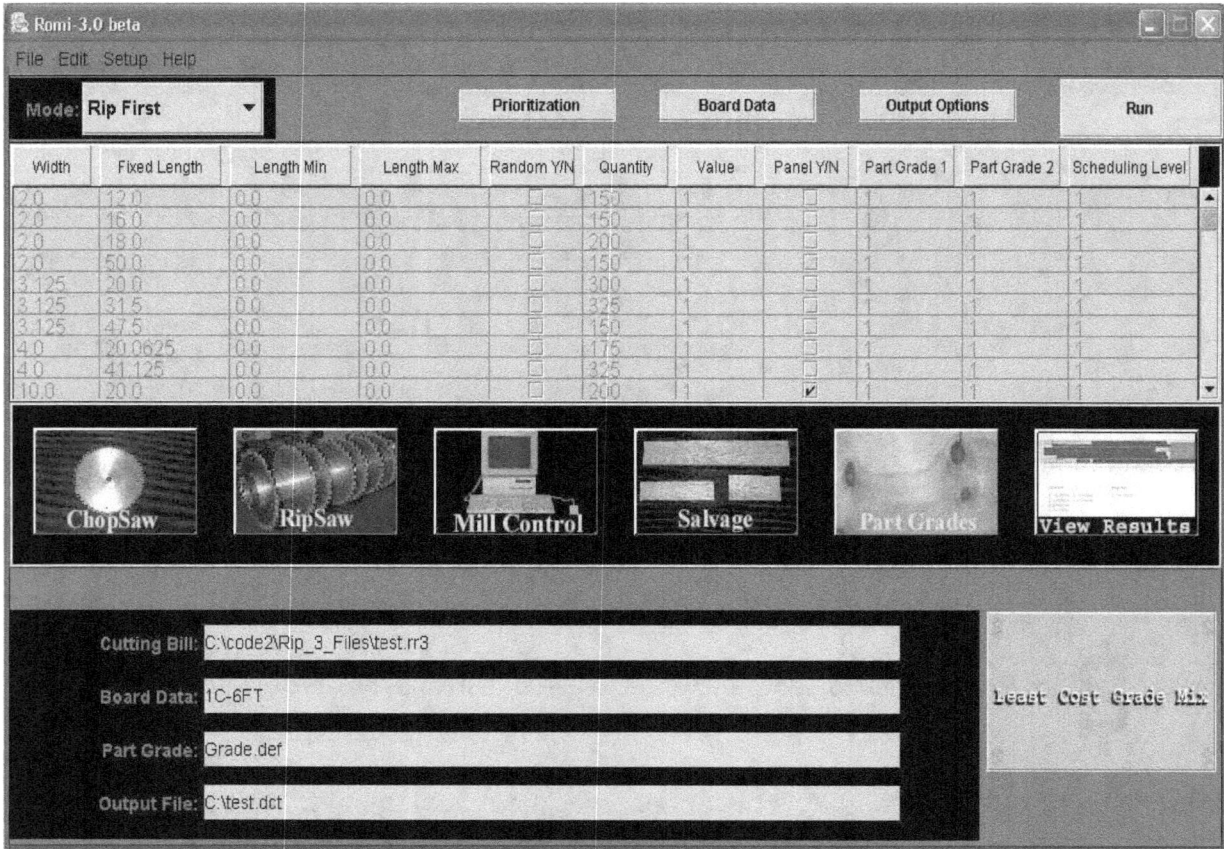

Width	Fixed Length	Length Min	Length Max	Random Y/N	Quantity	Value	Panel Y/N	Part Grade 1	Part Grade 2	Scheduling Level
2.0	12.0	0.0	0.0	☐	150	1	☐	1	1	1
2.0	16.0	0.0	0.0	☐	150	1	☐	1	1	1
2.0	18.0	0.0	0.0	☐	200	1	☐	1	1	1
2.0	50.0	0.0	0.0	☐	150	1	☐	1	1	1
3.125	20.0	0.0	0.0	☐	300	1	☐	1	1	1
3.125	31.5	0.0	0.0	☐	325	1	☐	1	1	1
3.125	47.5	0.0	0.0	☐	150	1	☐	1	1	1
4.0	20.0625	0.0	0.0	☐	175	1	☐	1	1	1
4.0	41.125	0.0	0.0	☐	325	1	☐	1	1	1
10.0	20.0	0.0	0.0	☐	200	1	☑	1	1	1

Figure 3.2a. Sample window showing table where the cutting bill information is entered and displayed.

3.2.1 Opening and Importing Cutting Bills

If you have previously used ROMI-RIP 2 or ROMI-CROSS, you can import your old cutting bills into ROMI-3. To do this, click *File* and then move the mouse to *Import*. Under the submenu, click *ROMI-Rip File (.rip)* or *ROMI-Cross File (.rmx .cut)*. You will see a file open window similar to that in Figure 3.2.1a.

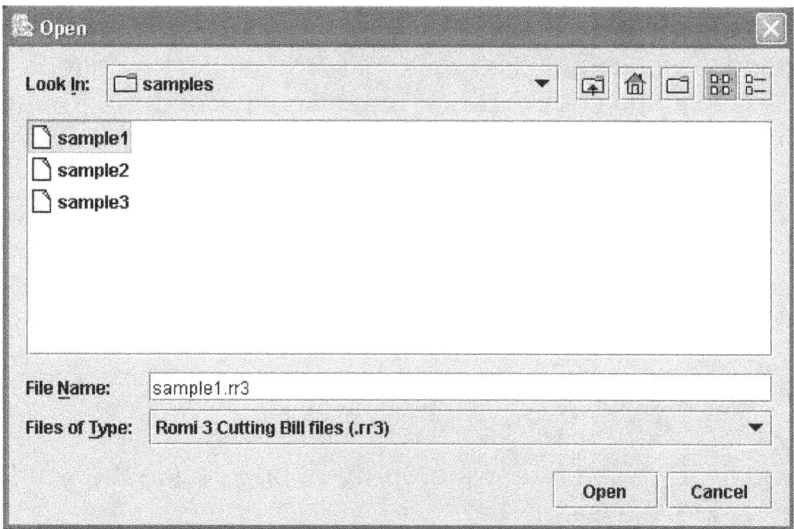
Figure 3.2.1a. ROMI-3 file chooser.

Navigate to where you have your files saved and double-click the file name. Once you have imported your cutting bill, you must save it in the ROMI-3 format that has the **.rr3** extension. To open a ROMI-3 file, use the same process as importing but click *File* and then click *Open*. You will again see the file open window shown in Figure 3.2.1a. Navigate to where you have your files saved and double-click the file name or click the file name and then click *Open*. Your settings will be loaded and the cutting bill will be displayed in the table.

3.2.2 Cutting Bill Editing

Data is entered into it just like an Excel spreadsheet. Hitting the *tab* key will move the cursor to the cell to the right of the current position. If you are in the last column, the cursor will advance to the first column of the next row. Hitting the *enter* key will move the cursor to the next row but will remain in the column you are currently editing. You also can use the arrow keys to move from cell to cell. To enter data into the table, move to the desired cell and begin typing. To edit a cell that contains data, move to the cell and hit the *backspace* key to erase the data from right to left, or double-click in the cell with the mouse to cause a blinking cursor to appear where you will start editing. There are two columns that must be handled differently: the Random Y/N and the Panel Y/N. In these columns, a check means yes and the absence of a check means no. You can click the box with the mouse or move to the cell and hit the space bar to toggle on or off.

Additional editing features include cut, copy, paste, and insert row. The cut and copy features are similar except that cut removes the data from the table whereas copy does not. To use the cut feature, select the items in the table by holding the mouse button down and dragging to highlight them. Then click *Edit* and then *Cut*; to copy, click *Edit* and then *Copy*. The items that were highlighted are now on the system clipboard. Now you can paste them to or from an Excel spreadsheet or to another position in the table. To paste, click the cell where you want the data to appear and click *Edit* and then *Paste*. If you cut or copy a cell with a check-box and then paste it into an Excel spreadsheet, the check-box data will be displayed as a 0, meaning no check, or a 1, meaning it is checked. Therefore, if you edit your cutting bill in Excel, enter a 0 if you do not want a check or 1 if you do. The last editing feature is insert row. To insert a row, click in the table where you want the blank row to be placed and click *Edit* and then *Insert Row*. One blank line will appear and the data below will be moved down one position. If you want to insert more than one blank row, click and drag the mouse downward, highlighting the same number of rows that you want to insert.

3.2.3 Cutting Modes

At the top of the main interface there is a drop-down box beside the word Mode that contains three items (Fig. 3.2.3a.).

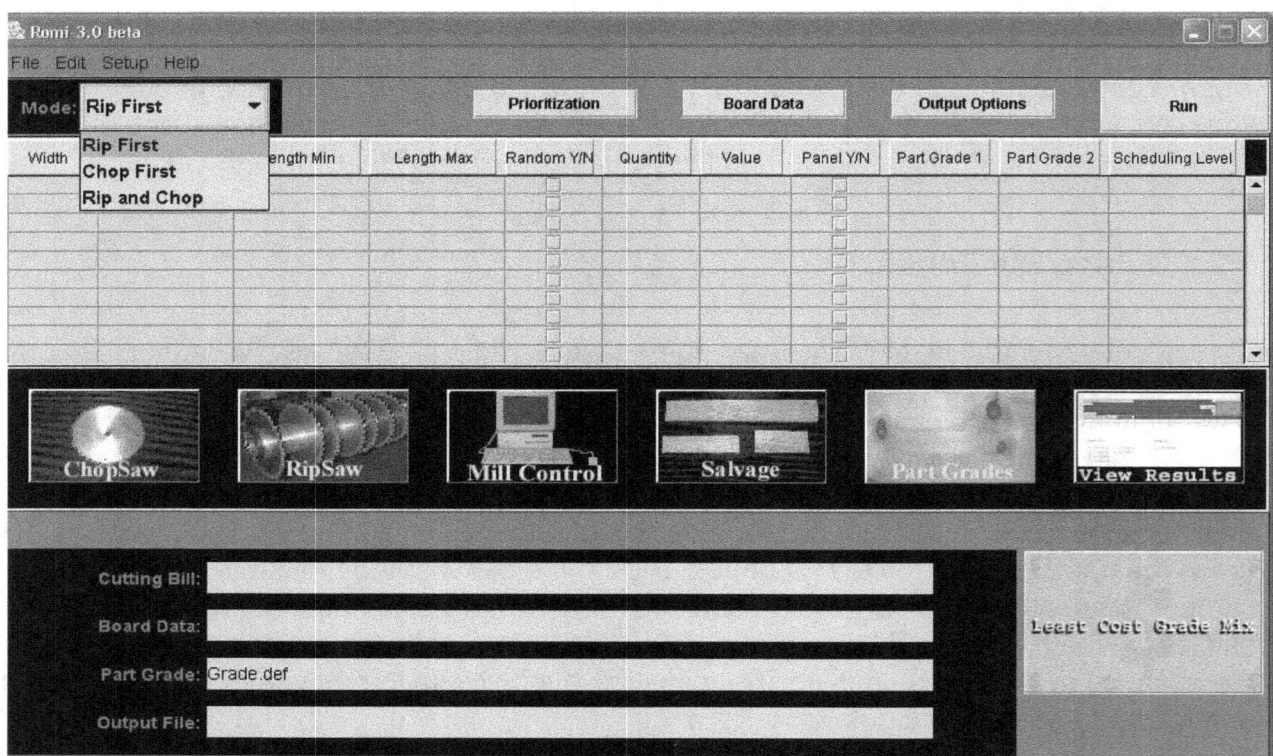

Figure 3.2.3a. ROMI-3 cutting modes.

The first option, *Rip First*, is modeled from the previous version of this software, ROMI-RIP 2, while the second option, *Chop First*, is modeled after ROMI-CROSS. The last option is *Rip* and *Chop,* which is not yet implemented.

24

3.2.4 Chopsaw Setup

The main interface contains six buttons with pictures. If you click on *Chopsaw* while you are in Rip First mode, you will bring up the window in Figure 3.2.4a.

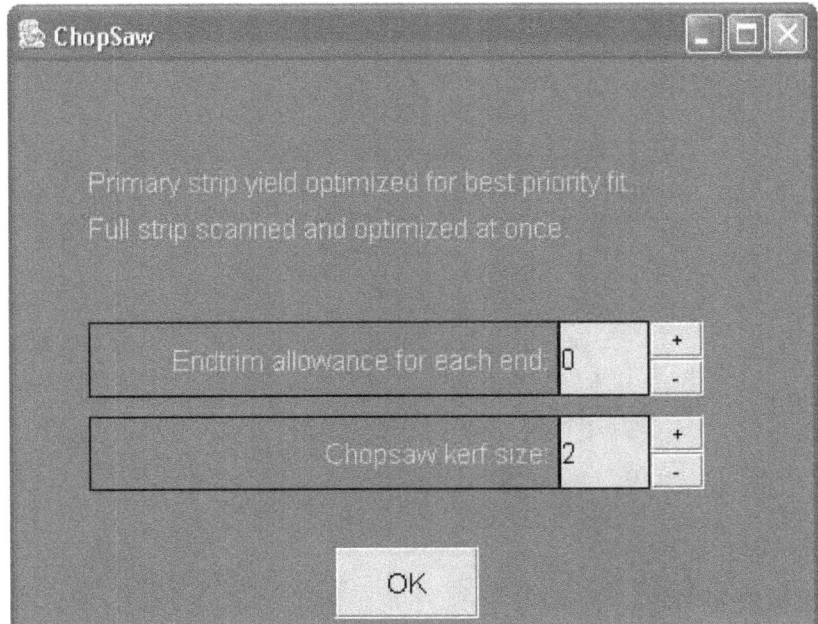

Figure 3.2.4a. Chopsaw setup window.

There are two settings you can modify in this window. Using the plus (+) and minus (-) buttons increases or decreases the values. The top setting indicates the amount of endtrim that you want to allow in sixteenths of an inch. A zero indicates that there will be no endtrimming. The bottom shows the amount of kerf (saw blade thickness) that you will account for. Figure 3.2.4a. shows no endtrim and a 1/8-inch kerf. When you are satisfied with the settings, click *OK* to close the window. You must save your cutting bill file before the settings will take affect.

3.2.5 Ripsaw Setup

Clicking on *Ripsaw* displays the window in Figure 3.2.5a.

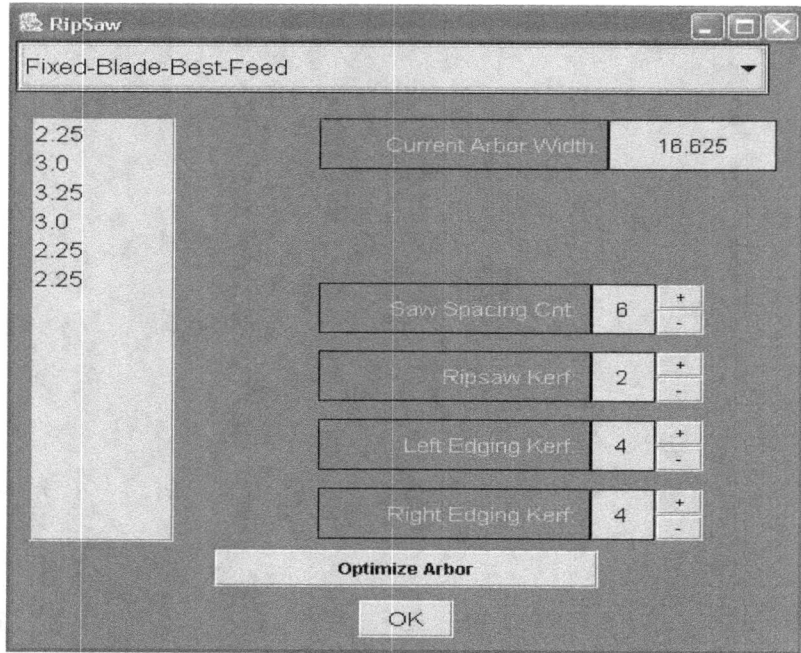

Figure 3.2.5a. Ripsaw setup window.

The box on the left side of the window shows the distance between the blades on the arbor. Adding these widths with a ripsaw kerf between spacings gives the total arbor width. This is displayed in the box next to the label Current Arbor Width. The plus and minus buttons beside Saw Spacing Cnt control the number of blades on the arbor. Increasing the number adds blades to the arbor and decreasing removes them. If you add a blade, it will appear in list of arbors with a value of zero. You must click on that number to bring up a pop-up window that allows you to select a width for the spacing (Fig. 3.2.5b.).

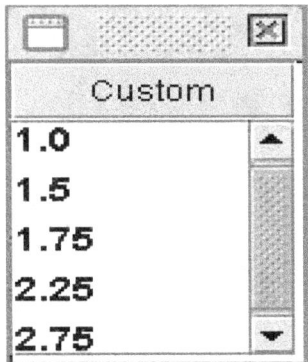

Figure 3.2.5b. Pop-up window for choosing spacings.

Click on a width to select or click *Custom* to enter your own width. Custom-width entry allows you to enter spacing widths that are not represented as a part size requirement in the cutting bill. This is especially useful if the cutting bill is composed primarily of panel parts and adding extra widths would improve strip and resulting part yield. The next three settings control the kerf and edgings and are represented in sixteenth-inch increments. Eight types of arbors are available in the ripsaw setup. Selection is from the drop-down box at the top of the window (Fig. 3.2.5c.).

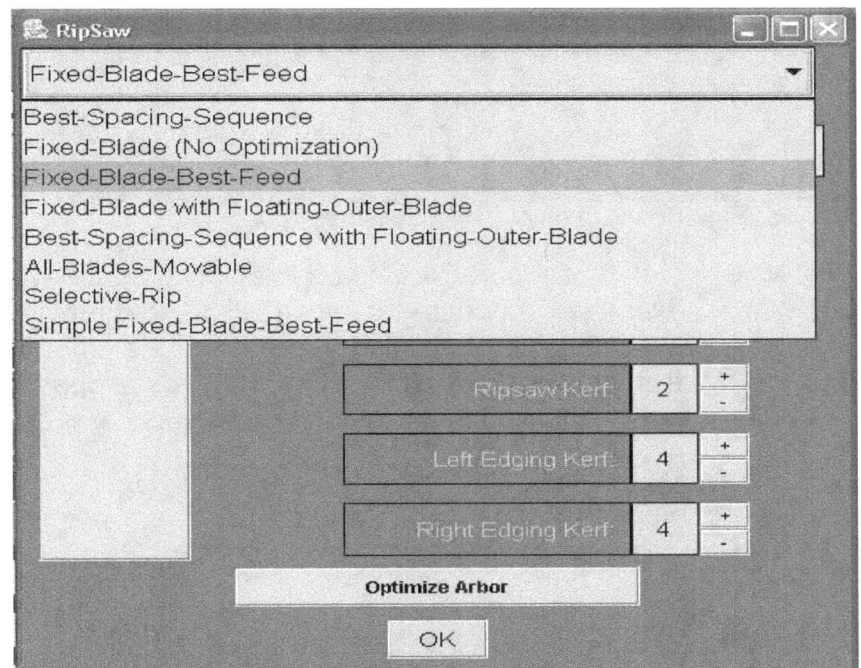

Figure 3.2.5c. Drop-down box showing types of arbors that may be used.

If you choose *Selective Rip* from the arbor drop-down box, two fields in the ripsaw settings window (Fig. 3.2.5d) are enabled. One field allows each blade on the arbor to be specified as fixed or movable. Clicking on the fixed or movable setting alternates between the two settings. The selective rip arbor does not allow adjacent blades to be specified as movable. If you require this feature, try the All-Blades-Movable arbor. The second field enabled for the movable-blade arbors, Saw Blade Proximity, allows the user to specify how close (in sixteenths of an inch) the moving blades on the arbor can come to adjacent blades. This setting usually is set to 12/16 (3/4) or 14/16 (7/8) of an inch and corresponds to the collar thickness and mechanical limits of gang-ripsaws.

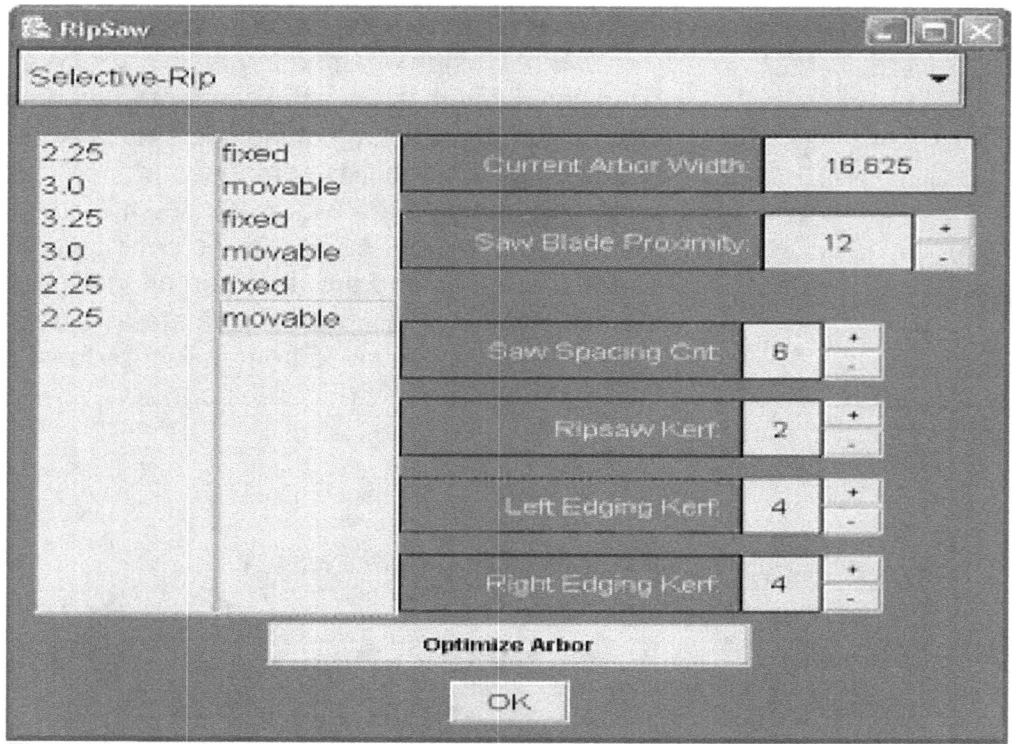

Figure 3.2.5d. Ripsaw setup using Selective-Rip arbor.

A new feature of ROMI-3 is *Optimize Arbor*. Clicking on this brings up the window in Figure 3.2.5e. The arbor optimizer examines your current cutting bill and determines the best possible arbor. The arbor optimizer takes a modified approach to the arbor design algorithm created by Gatchell (1996). Portions of the arbor optimizer were developed at North Carolina State University in cooperation with the USDA Forest Service.

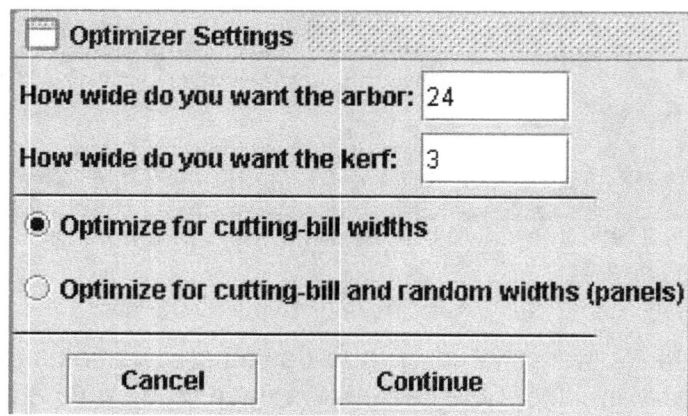

Figure 3.2.5e. Optimize Arbor setup window.

Enter your arbor width in inches, the kerf (saw blade thickness in sixteenths of an inch), and whether you want to optimize for solid widths only or widths that include panels. Then click *continue*. It may take several minutes to get the results depending on your computer's speed. When the optimizer is finished, you will see the arbor results window (Fig. 3.2.5f.).

28

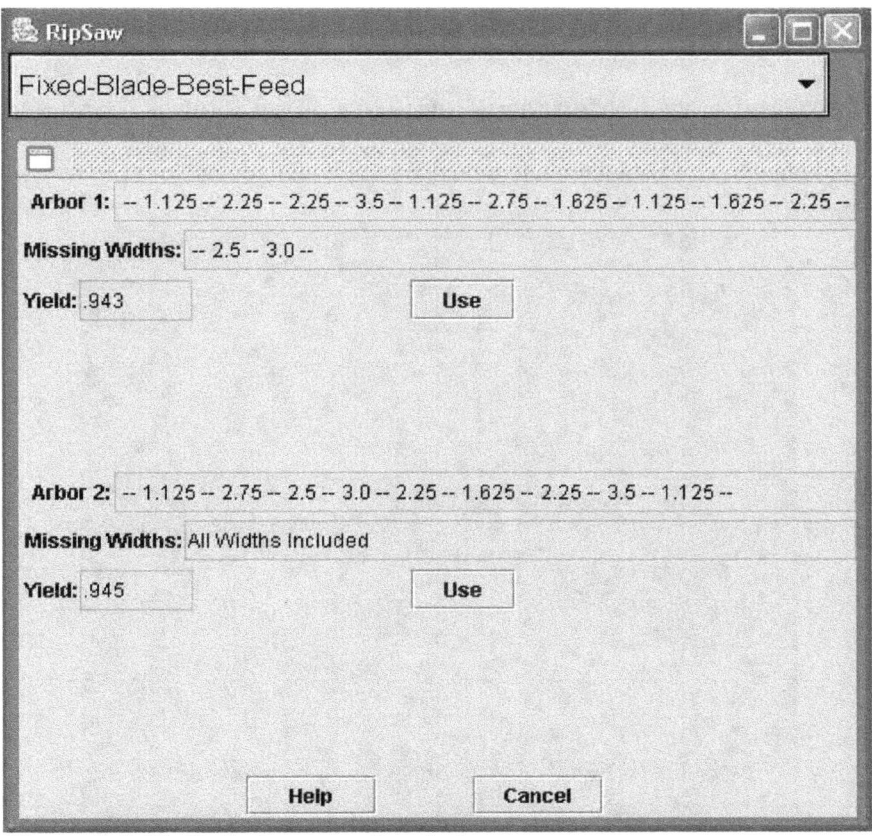

Figure 3.2.5f. Optimizer results window.

Depending on your options, you may have two arbors to choose from. If the optimizer gets a good yield while not including all of the widths in your cutting bill, it will be displayed followed by the arbor that includes all widths. You can examine the yield results and choose the arbor you want by clicking its *use* button.

3.2.6 Mill Control Setup

Clicking *Mill Control* in the main interface window brings up the Mill Control window (Fig. 3.2.6a.).

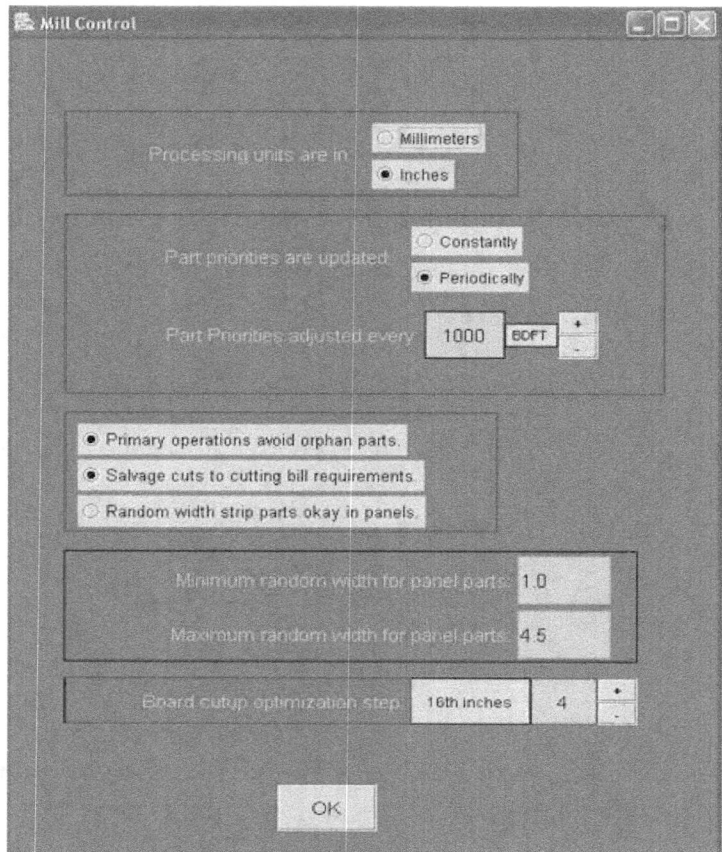

Figure 3.2.6a. Mill Control setup window.

The top two buttons allow you to toggle between using inches or millimeters throughout your setup. This button does not perform conversions. For example, 4/16 inch simply becomes 4 mm. Therefore, you should use the correct units throughout the entire process of building your cutting bill.

The part counts settings control how often part counts and priorities are updated when a dynamic prioritization method is used. Use the plus and minus buttons to change how often the count is updated or set it to zero to update constantly. The *Primary operations avoid orphan parts* and *Salvage cuts to cutting bill requirements* settings instruct the simulator not to cut excess primary parts without determining whether the area can be salvage ripped to obtain a narrower cutting bill part. The *Random width strip parts okay in panels* setting should be used if you are not concerned with what width parts are used to make up panels. If you are using a moving-blade arbor, enable this setting to take full advantage of the arbor. You also can use the next fields to set the minimum and maximum widths for making up a panel. The last setting, *Board cutup optimization step*, does not correspond to a real-world rough-mill setting. For fixed-blade-best-feed and selective-rip arbors, this setting controls how many feed positions are examined per inch of arbor width. For example, a cutup optimization step of 4 would examine one feeding position every 4/16 inch. For a 24-inch-wide arbor, ROMI-3 would examine 96 ((24 * 16) ÷ 4) feed positions. For the all-blades-movable arbor, the setting controls how many random widths are examined by the arbor. A cutup optimization step of 4/16 would examine widths to the nearest quarter inch, while a setting of 2/16 would examine widths to the nearest eighth inch. Note that the smaller the optimization step becomes, the longer the simulation run time.

3.2.7 Salvage Parts Setup

Clicking *Salvage Parts* from the main interface brings up the window in Figure 3.2.7a.

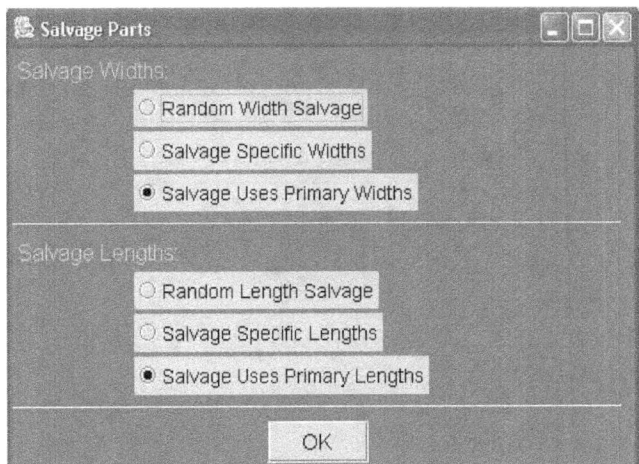

Figure 3.2.7a. Salvage Parts setup window.

There are three possible settings each for the salvage widths and lengths. *Random Width* or *Length Salvage* allows the program to randomly pick the parts it tries to obtain from the salvage. Choosing *Salvage Specific Widths* or *Lengths* enables a box that allows you to choose the widths or lengths manually (Fig. 3.2.7b.).

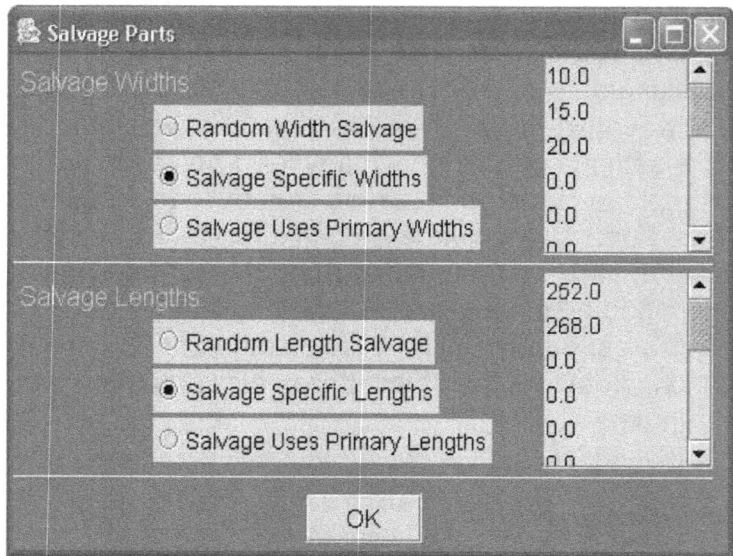

Figure 3.2.7b. Salvage settings using specific widths and lengths.

To edit a width or length, click on it to bring up the window in Figure 3.2.7c.

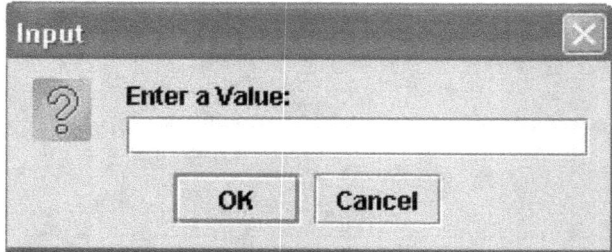

Figure 3.2.7c. Window used to enter specific widths and lengths.

Enter the value you want and click *OK*. To delete a width, click on it and enter 0 in the window. The last option, *Salvage Uses Primary Widths* or *Lengths*, allows ROMI-3 to try to obtain salvage from the widths or lengths found in the cutting bill.

3.2.8 Prioritization Setup

When processing to meet a cutting bill's requirements, the goal is to cut all required part sizes from a minimal amount of lumber while generating a minimal number of excess parts. This is made more difficult by variations in lumber grades and dimensions. To address this problem in simulation, seven part prioritization strategies are available ranging from simple to complex (Thomas 1996). The simple methods prioritize parts based on area. Complex methods generate part priorities based on each part's size and current required quantity. The complex methods are dynamic in that a part priority can be updated continually as parts are cut and current quantity decreases. As the quantity requirements for a part size are met, emphasis shifts to other sizes. Deciding on the combination of parts to cut from a board is based on maximizing the total weighted area of parts for each board.

Clicking Prioritization on the main interface brings up the window in Figure 3.2.8a. Use this window to select the type of strategy you want to use.

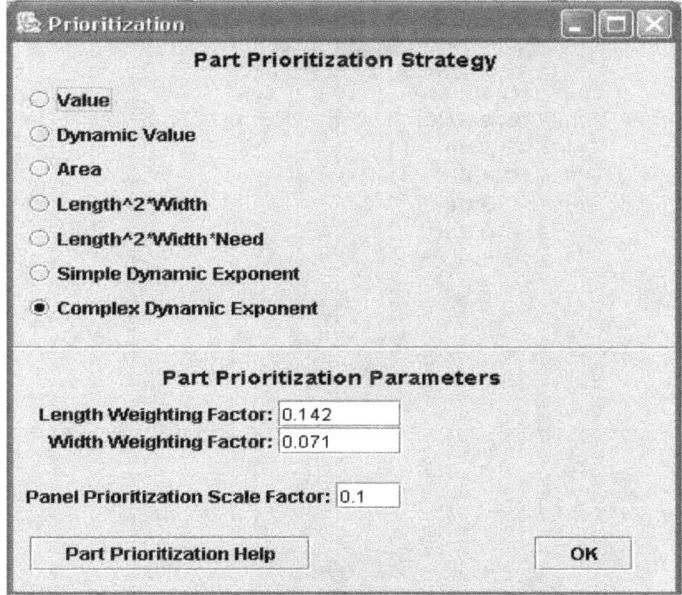

Figure 3.2.8a. Prioritization setup window.

3.2.9 Part Scheduling and Replacement

A scheduling problem occurs when the number of different part sizes in a cutting bill exceeds a rough mill's sorting capacity. Decisions must be made as to which parts will be processed first and the order in which the remaining parts will be processed as initial part requirements are met. ROMI 3 allows this scheduling with the *Scheduling Level* variable (Fig. 3.2a) associated with each part. Parts with a level of 1 are cut first. Parts with a level of 2 are used to replace level 1 parts as their requirements are met. Parts with larger level values are entered in sequence. The total number of parts with a level 1 is the total number of different sorts that are available.

4. Datafile Selection

Clicking *Board Data* from the main ROMI-3 window brings up the Datafile chooser window (Fig. 4a.). This is where you choose files containing digitized boards from the databank. The top box shows the available board files and the bottom box shows the selected board files to use. To choose a board file, double-click the name of the file and it will be displayed in the bottom box. You can use multiple files and the same file twice. To remove a file, double-click the name in the bottom box. When you have the data files that you want, click *OK*.

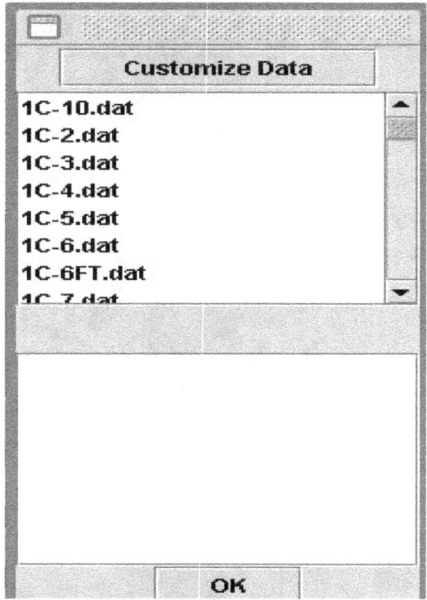

Figure 4a. Datafile chooser window.

4.1 Creating Custom Grade Mix and Specified Files

You can create custom board data files by clicking on *Customize Data*. This will start the *MakeFile* program (Fig. 4.1a.) that allows you to specify a grade mix or choose individual boards for your simulations. With the makefile program you can create board data sets that closely resemble the characteristics (width and length distribution, grade mix) of actual lumber being processed in your rough mill. As mentioned earlier, board data included with ROMI-3 is from the 1998 Data Bank for Kiln-Dried Red Oak Lumber (Gatchell et al. 1998) and is graded to 1998 NHLA rules (NHLA 1998). See Appendix II for additional information on the lumber data.

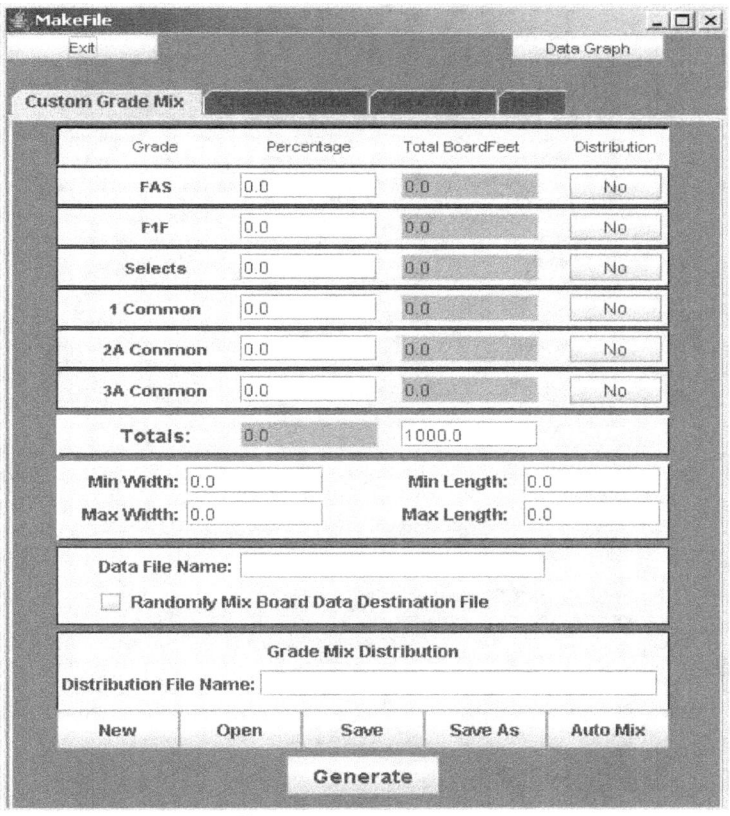
Figure 4.1a. Makefile program.

4.1.1 Custom Grade Mix

Custom Grade Mix is the default tab that is selected when makefile is started. This allows you to specify percentages of desired lumber grades from the lumber data bank. The percentage column is where you specify the percentage of each grade. If you want 50 percent No. 1 Common, select the cell next to 1 Common and enter **50**; if you want 20 percent 2A Common, select the cell next to 2A Common and enter **20**. The total percentage for all grades is displayed on the totals line and must add to 100 before the file can be generated. As you change the percentages you will see the Totals field change. If you exceed 100 percent, the total number will change to red, indicating the percentage is too high. Under the Total Board Feet column, the default sample size is 1,000 board feet. To change the sample size, select the cell and enter the amount of board feet you want. When the sample size is changed, Makefile automatically recalculates the total board feet needed for each grade based on the percentage entered. It also is possible to specify board minimum and maximum width and lengths. Both length and width are measured in inches to the nearest 1/4 inch. In the example in Figure 4.1.1a., we specified a 2,500 board-foot sample consisting of a 30 percent No. 1 Common, 70 percent No. 2A Common grade mix with no minimum or maximum length or width.

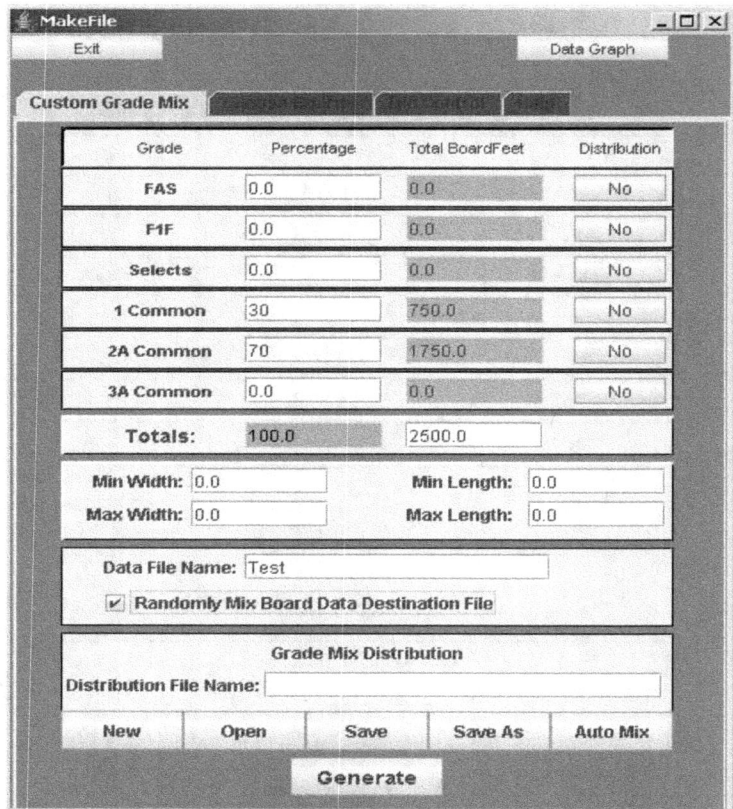

Figure 4.1.1a. Makefile showing a sample grade mix.

A distribution editor is available for those who want to match a specific width and/or length distribution. For each grade, a distribution of as many as 20 size ranges can be specified. There is a button for each grade under the Distribution column that is labeled *No* by default. Clicking any of the *Distribution* buttons will bring up the window in Figure 4.1.1b.

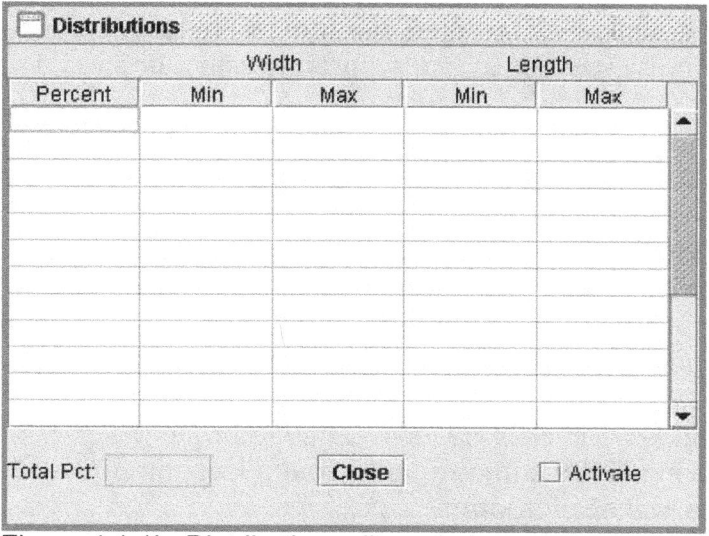

Figure 4.1.1b. Distribution editor window.

Click on the percent or length and width cells to edit them. As you add percentages, they are added and displayed in the Total Pct: box (Fig. 4.1.1c). The total must add to 100 percent. Note that these distributions are a percent of a percentage. Thus, if 30 percent of the sample is No. 1 Common and 20 percent of the No. 1 Common distribution is to be 6 to 7 inches wide, we are referring to 6 percent of the total sample size. After a distribution has been defined, it must be activated before it can be used. To do this, click the *Activate check box* that will place a check in the box (Fig. 4.1.1c.).

	Width		Length	
Percent	Min	Max	Min	Max
30	4.0	5.0		
40	5.0	6.0		
20	6.0	7.0		
10	7.0	8.0		

Total Pct: 100.0   **Close**   ☑ Activate

Figure 4.1.1c. Sample data in Distribution editor.

If you choose not to use the distribution, remove the check from the box. When you are satisfied with your distribution, click *Close* to return to the main screen. If you enabled the distribution, the button will say *Yes* in red. All grades with a defined distribution will say *Yes*.

Now you must enter a name for the data file in the Destination File Name box (Fig. 4.1.1a.). Note that it does not need the .dat extension. If you want the boards in the resulting file to be randomly mixed, place a check in the box next to the Randomly Mix Board Data Destination File label. To create the data file, click *Generate*. Depending on the speed of your computer and the size of the file created, you will see a box that says Generation Successful. Click *OK* and your file will appear in the list of available data files (Fig. 4a.). You have now created a data file and can exit the Makefile program or save your grade-mix settings. Click *Save* to bring up the file chooser. Navigate to where you want to save your current settings and click *Save*. You can return to Makefile at any time and open the grade mix by clicking *Open* and navigating to the location of your file and opening it. Click *Exit* to close the Makefile program.

4.1.2 Choose Boards

ROMI-3 and Makefile allow you to create a data file that contains boards from several different data files. Clicking *Choose Boards* at the top of the main window will bring up the window in Figure 4.1.2a. Notice that the left list shows all of the available data files. A single click on any of the data files will open it and display all of the boards in that file (Fig. 4.1.2b.).

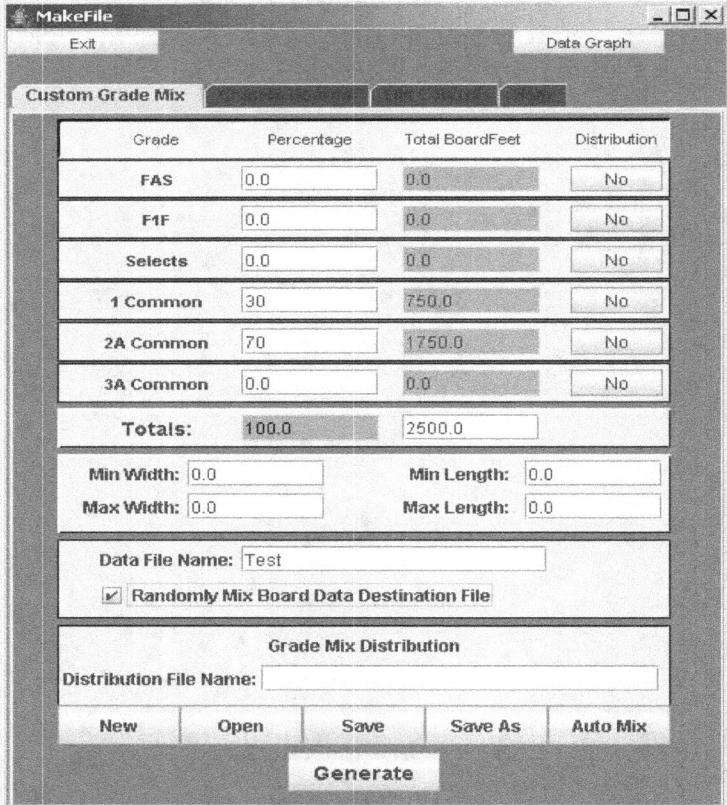

Figure 4.1.2a. Choose Boards window.

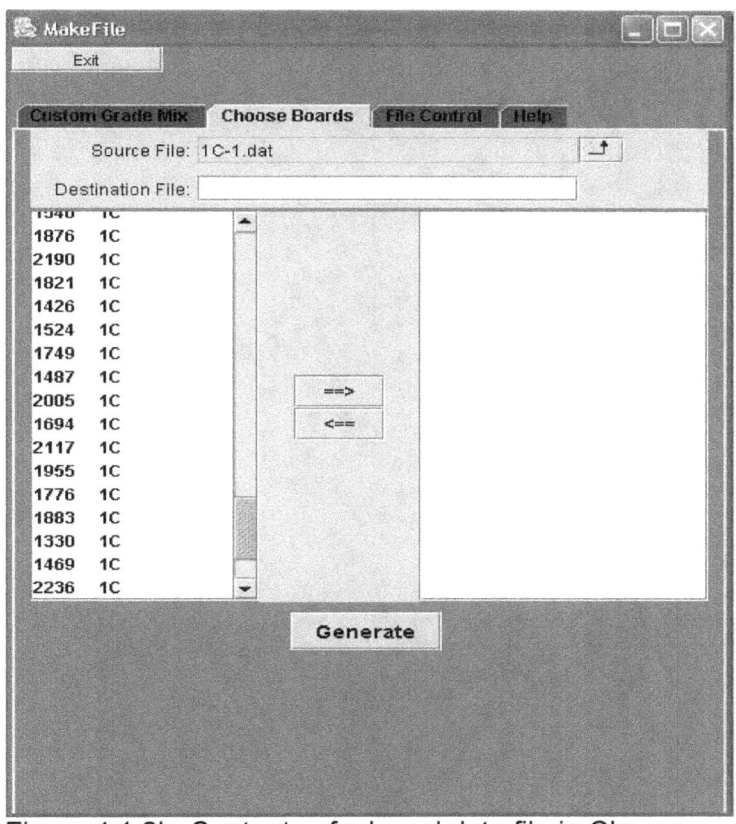

Figure 4.1.2b. Contents of a board data file in Choose Boards window.

As seen in Figure 4.1.2b., the source file name is 1C-1.dat. The left list shows the individual boards and grade in the 1C-1.dat file. To choose a board, double-click it or click once and then click the *arrow* button. You also can choose more than one board at a time by clicking a board to highlight it and then holding down *shift* and clicking another board in the list to highlight everything between the two selected boards. Now click the arrow button to move them to the other list. To choose multiple boards that do not follow each other in the list, hold down *ctrl* and click each board that you want. When you are ready, click the *arrow* button to place them in the list on the right. You can use boards from other board data files by clicking the up arrow ⬆ beside the source file box to the list of data files. Repeat the process to choose individual boards. The result should be similar to that in Figure 4.1.2c.

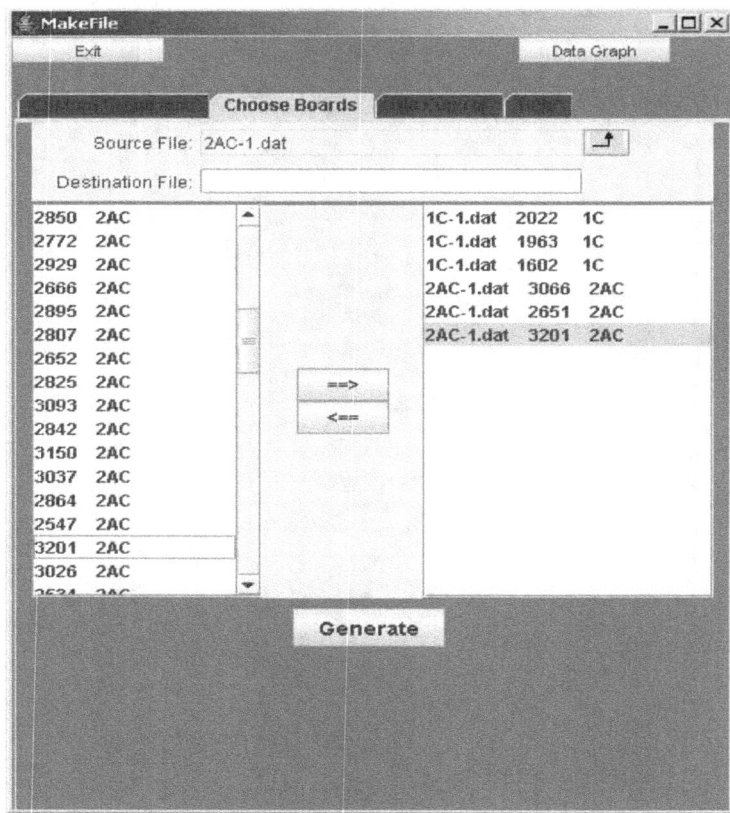

Figure 4.1.2c. Selected boards in Choose
Boards window.

The list on the right also contains the data file name that the boards came from as well
as the board number and grade. When you have all of the boards that you want, type
a file name in the Destination File box and click *Generate*. Depending on the speed of
your computer and the size of the file created, you will see a box that says Generation
Successful. Click *OK* and your file will be included in the list of available data files
(Fig. 4a.). You now have created your data file and can click *Exit*.

4.1.3 File Control

Clicking the File Control tab brings up the window in Figure 4.1.3a. The list contains only
data files that are generated by the user. To delete a file, click the file name to highlight it
and then click *Delete*.

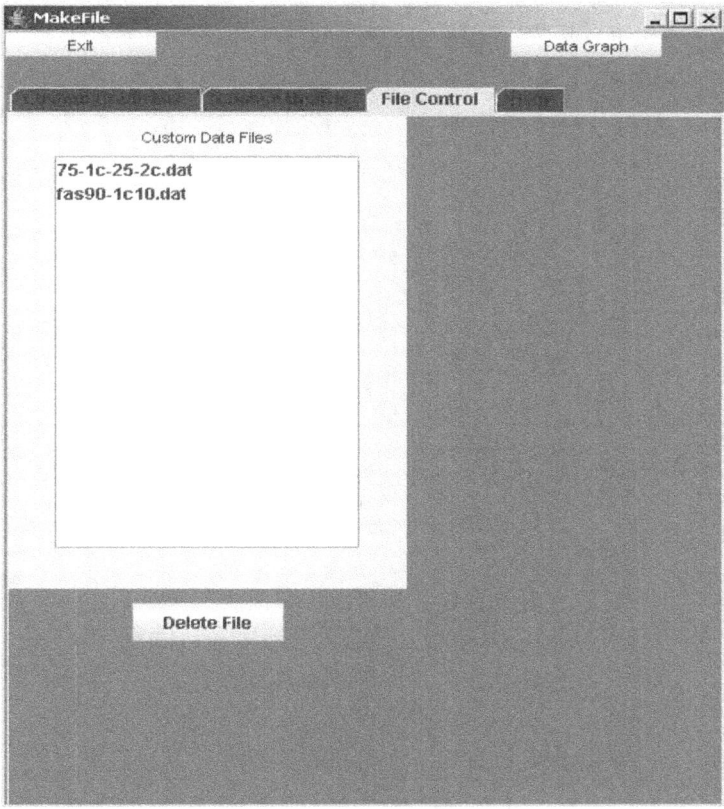

Figure 4.1.3a. File Control window.

4.2 Data Graph

Clicking *Data Graph* will bring up the window in Figure 4.2.a. Data Graph allows you to choose any data file and tallies all of the boards by width and length. This can be used to check the distribution of a data file to ensure that the desired boards are included.

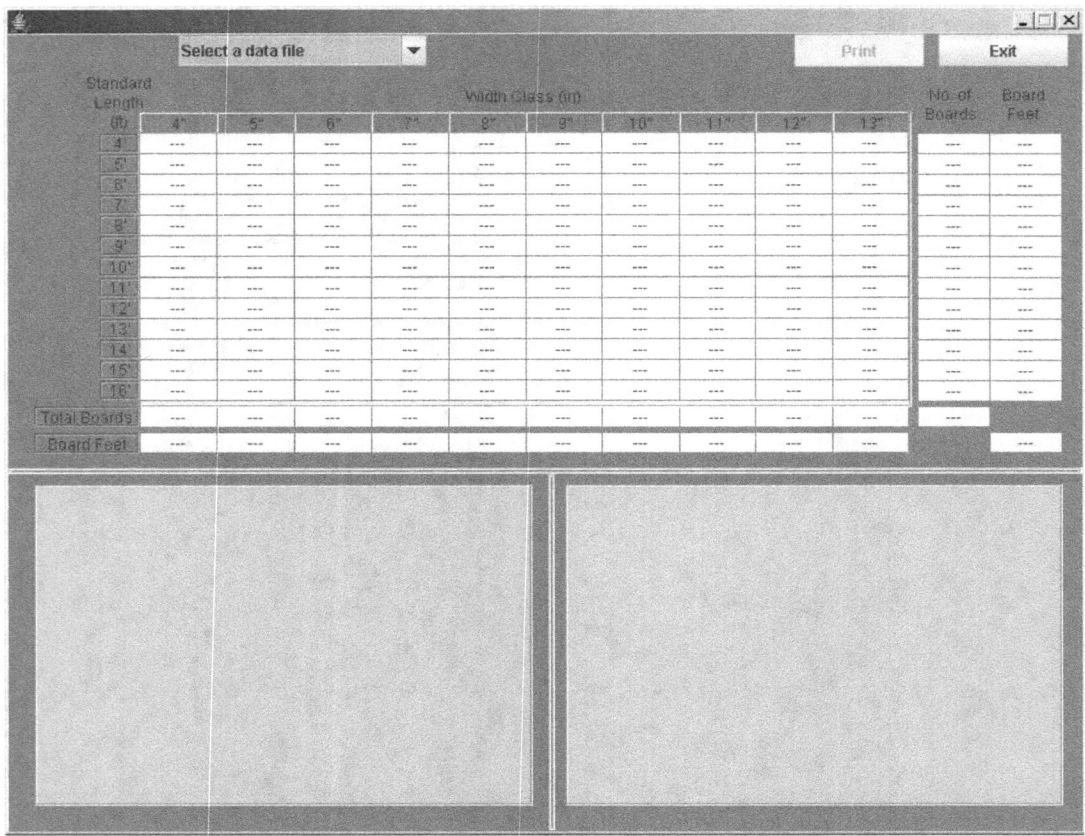

Figure 4.2.a. Data Graph window.

To view a data file, choose the file name from the drop-down box at the top of the screen. The chart now displays the width and length of every board in the file. The two bar graphs at the bottom of the screen are a representation of the chart at the top (Fig. 4.2.b.). You can print the current data file information by clicking *Print*. Click *Exit* to close the window.

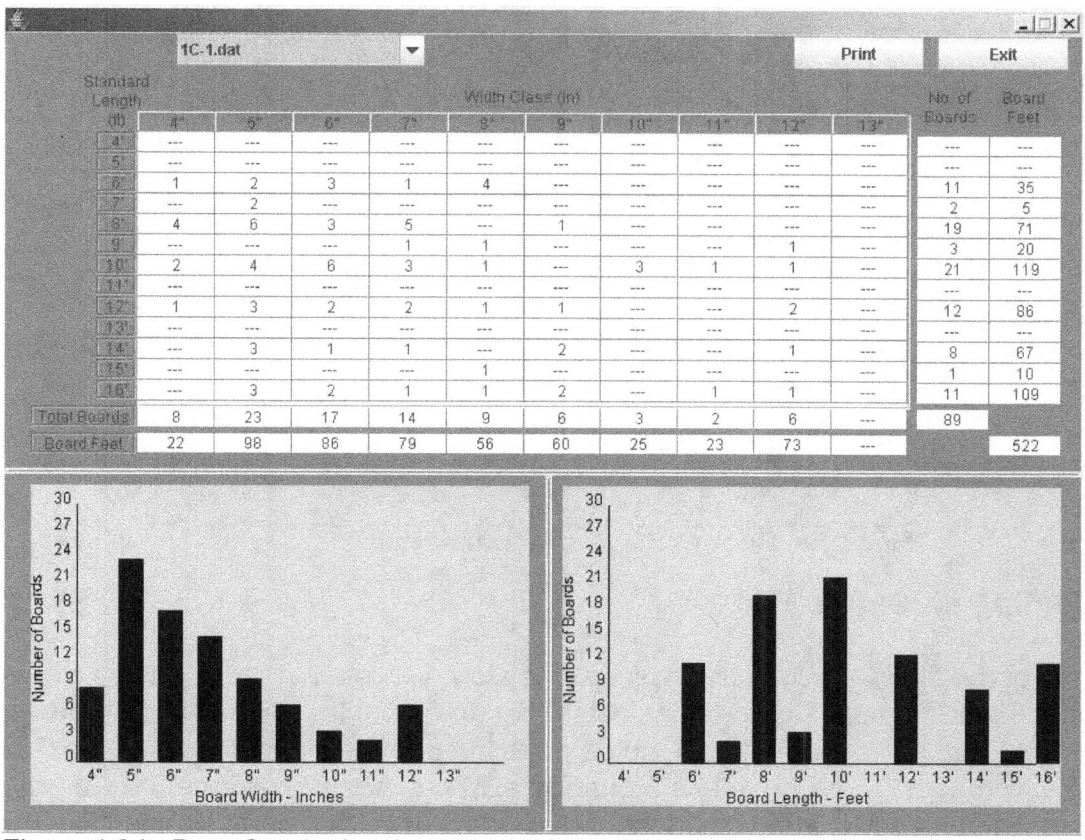

Figure 4.2.b. Data Graph showing board information.

5. Output Options

ROMI-3 provides several output types for applications such as spreadsheets, least-cost-grade-mix programs, and flow simulation. The Configure Output Options window (Fig. 5a.) allows you to specify a filename for your results, select output types, and set up length and width ranges for summary reports. Click *Output Options* in the main ROMI-3 interface (Fig. 2.4a.) to bring up the Configure Output Options window (Fig. 5a.).

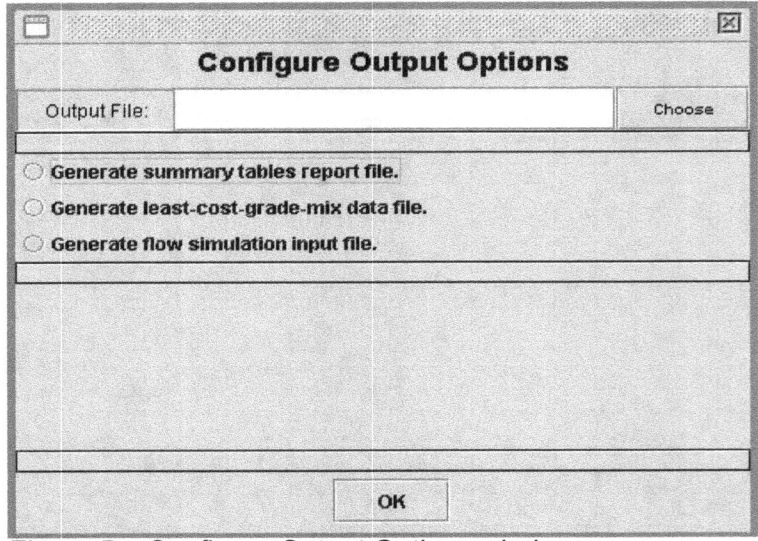

Figure 5a. Configure Output Options window.

5.1 Selecting an Output File

The name of the file in which your output will be stored is listed at the top of the screen in the Output File entry box. Figure 5a indicates that an output file has not yet been selected. To specify an output file, select the button next to the entry box that says *Choose*. This will bring up a file chooser like the one in Figure 3.1a. You can specify where the file will be located by entering a name or writing over an existing file. After choosing the file name, click *Save As*.

5.2 Summary Tables

Summary tables contain part counts, surface areas, and yields for primary and salvage in user-defined size (width and length) categories. These tables are especially useful when cutting to random sizes. Clicking *Generate summary tables report file* turns on and off the generation of summary tables (Fig. 5a.). This option is off by default. If you choose to use summary tables, you also must check the width and length range settings. These are discussed in detail in Section 5.4.; examples of summary table output are included in Section 7.2.

5.3 Flow Simulation Output

ROMI-3 can generate step-by-step processing information for each board, including the number of strips, primary and salvage parts, primary crosscuts and rips, and salvage crosscuts (Stiess 1995). This information can be used as an input for complete rough-mill flow simulation. Select *Generate flow simulation input file* (Fig. 5a.) to turn on and off flow simulation file generation. This option is off by default.

5.4 Length and Width Ranges

For purposes of data presentation, it is necessary to specify width ranges and, in the case of random length processing, length ranges. Fifteen width and length ranges allow yield information to be grouped and subtotaled according to your interest. The default width ranges editor is shown in Figure 5.4a.

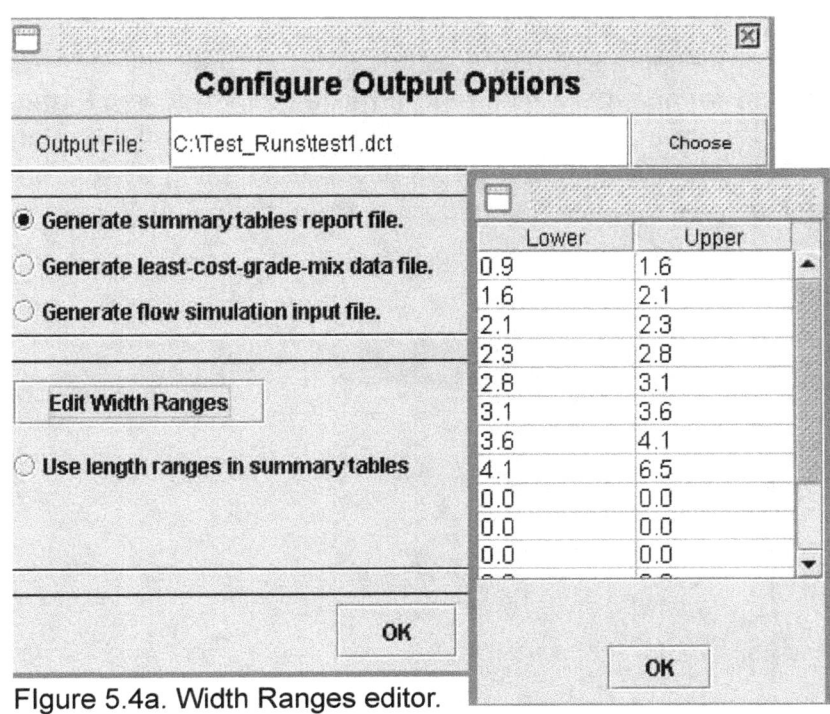

Figure 5.4a. Width Ranges editor.

The editing steps are the same for both range types. To modify width or length ranges, click the button *Edit Width Ranges or Edit Length Ranges* and then double-click in the cell and change the value (Fig. 5.4a.). It is good practice not to use primary part widths or lengths to begin or end a range as this may result in inaccurate subtotals. For example, to specify a range that includes the two widths 1.5 and 2.0 inches, specify a lower range value of 1.45 and an upper value of 2.05. Length Ranges allow you to group random-length results by length groupings. If length ranges are turned off, a subtotal in the summary tables is created for every different part length produced. The result can be extremely large tables even for medium-size runs. If there are too many lengths, the summary program cannot process them all. When you are satisfied with your settings, click *OK*.

6. Starting the Analysis

All of the preceding work has been in preparation for producing rough-dimension parts from your lumber grade mix using the cutting bill and processing options. This step can take several minutes to hours to complete depending on the size of your cutting bill, processing options, and computer speed. In most cases, the simulation analysis requires less that an hour.

Your cutting bill and processing settings are checked automatically for errors before each run. If errors are found, you will see the error report window in Figure 6a. Errors should be corrected before continuing. If you suspect that something might be wrong with your cutting bill or processing settings while you are setting up a simulation, you can run error checking manually by selecting *File* from the ROMI-3 main window (Fig. 2.4a.) and clicking *Check for Errors*.

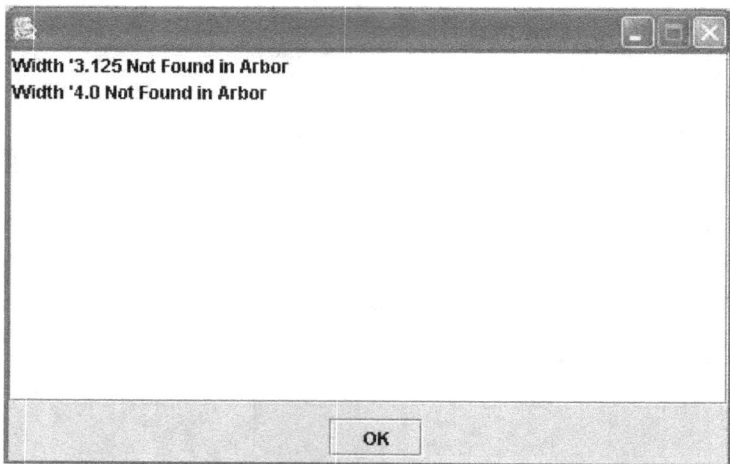

Figure 6a. Example Error Report window.

There are two ways to run the analysis: interactive or batch. Note: You should run each cutting bill in interactive mode prior to running in batch mode to ensure that all settings are adjusted correctly. Running the analysis interactively is the easiest but ties the computer up for potentially long periods. Running the analysis in batch mode is slightly more difficult but allows you to run more than one analysis at a time. Batch mode also allows you to run the analysis at night or when you will be away from your computer for some time.

6.1 Interactive Mode

To start the analysis, click *Run* in the main interface window (Fig. 2.4a.). If you failed to select any board data files for processing or have any other errors, ROMI-3 will inform you. A processing window will open and list board numbers and dimensions as they are processed. ROMI-3 stops processing automatically when all cutting bill requirements have been met or all boards in the selected data files have been processed (Fig. 6.1a.).

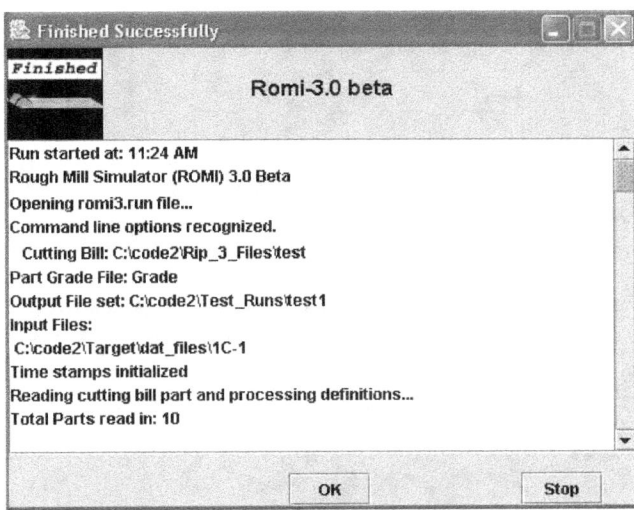

Figure 6.1a. Example Run window.

6.2 Batch Mode

ROMI-3 has extensive batch-run capabilities. This is useful if you have several large simulations you would like to run overnight. Note: You should run each cutting bill in interactive mode prior to running in batch mode to ensure that all settings are correct. To start the batch mode editor, click *Setup* from the ROMI-3 main window (Fig. 2.4.) and then *Batch Job* to open the window in Figure 6.2a.

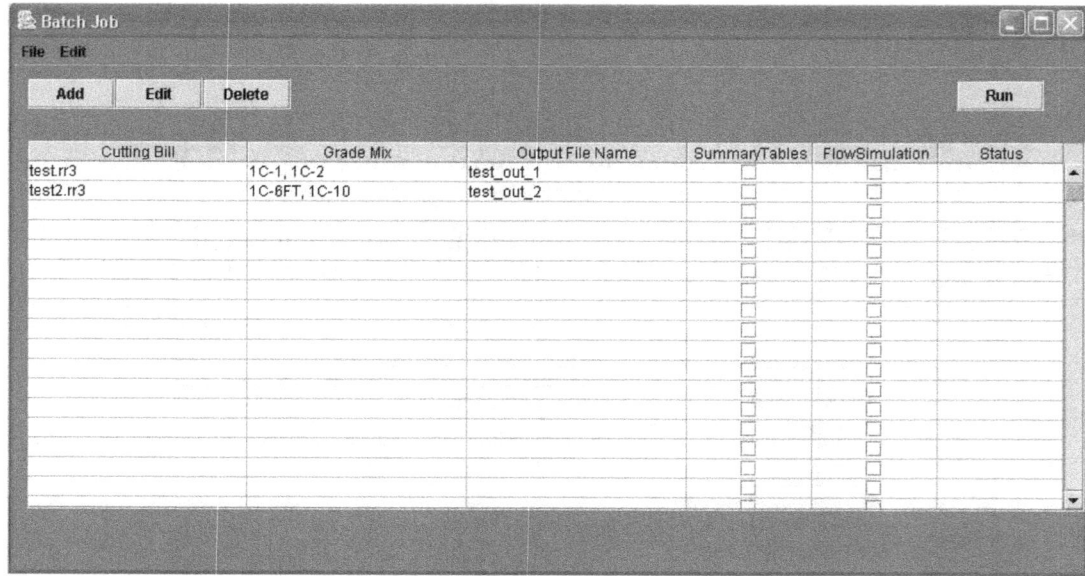

Figure 6.2a. Example Batch Job Editor window.

To set up a batch run, click *Add* to bring up a file chooser like that in Figure 3.1a. This is where you select your cutting bill file. A window will open that shows all possible board data files. It is identical to the data file chooser in the main ROMI-3 interface. The last window that opens allows you to choose where you want to store the output of the run. You can turn on summary tables but they must first be set up in the main interface. Flow simulation also can be turned on if desired.

Click *Add* again and repeat the previous steps for additional runs. You need to ensure that the output file names are not duplicated as this will overwrite your results with the last run to use the file. If you need to change the setup, click the desired cell and click *Edit*. This opens the window for that cell that allows you to change the contents. *Delete* is used to remove an entire row from the list. Click the first cell of the row containing the cutting bill name and then *Delete*. All of the settings will be adjusted.

Another feature of the batch editor is the ability to copy and paste the cells that already contain data. To use this featu*re, click a single cell or highlight a group of cells. Then click Edit on the menu bar and then Copy.* Now click the cell where you want to start pasting and click the *Edit* menu again and then *Paste*. You now see an exact copy of your data.

The last feature of the batch editor is the ability to save your batch file setup and reopen it at any time. If you want to save your current setup, click *File* and then *Save*. You will see a file chooser and can navigate to where you want to save your file. Then click *Save*, which saves the batch files with a .btc extension. To open this file or any other, click *File* and then *Open*. Your settings will be displayed in the editor.

To start the batch run, click *Run*. Notice that each cell in the status column (Fig. 6.2a.) now contains one of three values: Waiting, Running, or Finished. When all of the runs have completed, a window opens telling you that it is complete. Click *OK* to return to the editor. Closing the editor window returns you to the ROMI-3 main interface.

7. Simulation Results

ROMI-3 provides the user with many result types for each simulation. These include summary tables, yields and processing requirements, cutting bill reports, board plots, and input data for flow simulation analysis. The last data type is intended to be used only by other applications. The other report types are intended to be printed out or examined using the Viewer in ROMI-3. To run the Viewer, click *View Results* in the main ROMI-3 interface (Fig. 2.4a) to open the Viewer window.

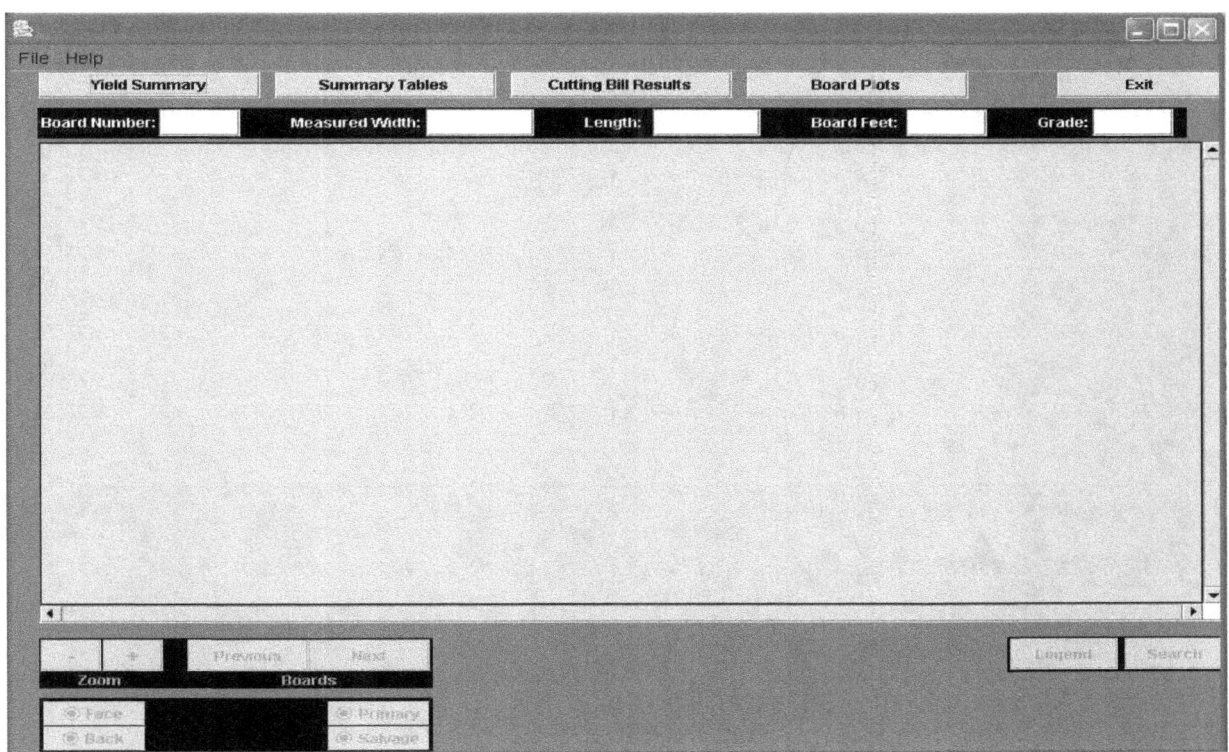

Figure 7a. Results Viewer main window.

When the viewer is first opened, the screen is grey until you open a file and select a result type using the buttons at the top of the window (Fig. 7a.). To select a results type, click *File* and then *Open*. You will see a file chooser like that in Figure 3.1a. Select the file that contains the ROMI-3 output that you wish to view. To view results, select one of the result buttons at the top of the window. When you are finished viewing and printing summaries and board plots, click *Exit* to leave the viewer.

7.1 Yield Summary Results

To view yield summary results, click *Yield Summary* at the top of the window (Fig. 7a.). The first part of the yield report summarizes the processing options used in the analysis. Items such as arbor type, kerf sizes, and prioritization settings are listed. Yield summary tables (Fig. 7.1a.) follow the processing options.

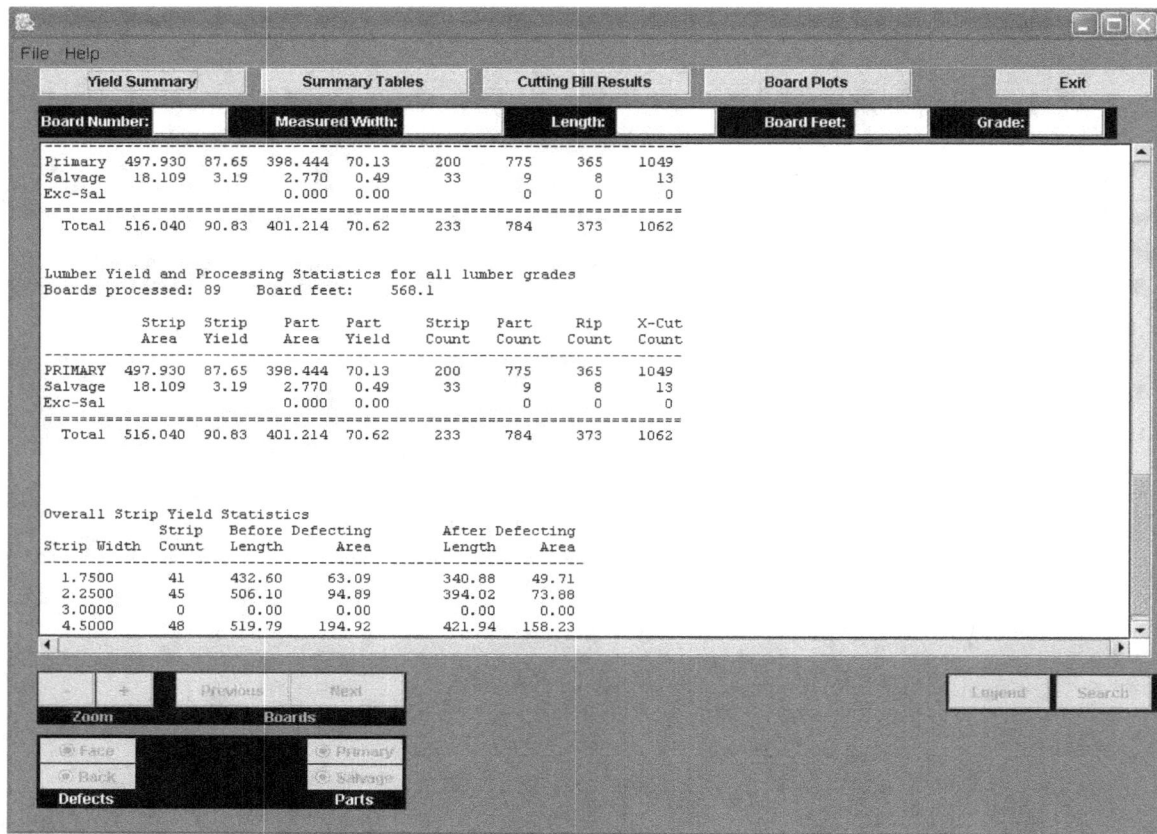

Figure 7.1a. Example Yield Summary Results.

These tables list for each grade processed and all grades combined the yield and processing requirements (numbers of strips, parts, rips, and crosscuts) for primary, salvage, excess primary, and excess salvage yield categories.

7.2 Summary Table Results

Summary tables provide detailed information on parts and yield. They list the number of parts generated, surface area, and percentage of parts by user-defined width and length groupings. Select *Summary Tables* from the top of the viewer window (Fig. 7a.). The first part of the summary table report lists the processing options and yield summaries discussed in Section 7.1. Because summary tables can be large, you may want to print them for easier examination. Select *File* and then *Print* to print summary table results (Fig. 7a.). All summary tables for an input file are placed in a single output file with the extension .sum. There are six summary tables that describe yield distributions. The first three tables give the distributions based on surface area. A sample is shown in Figure 7.2a.

50

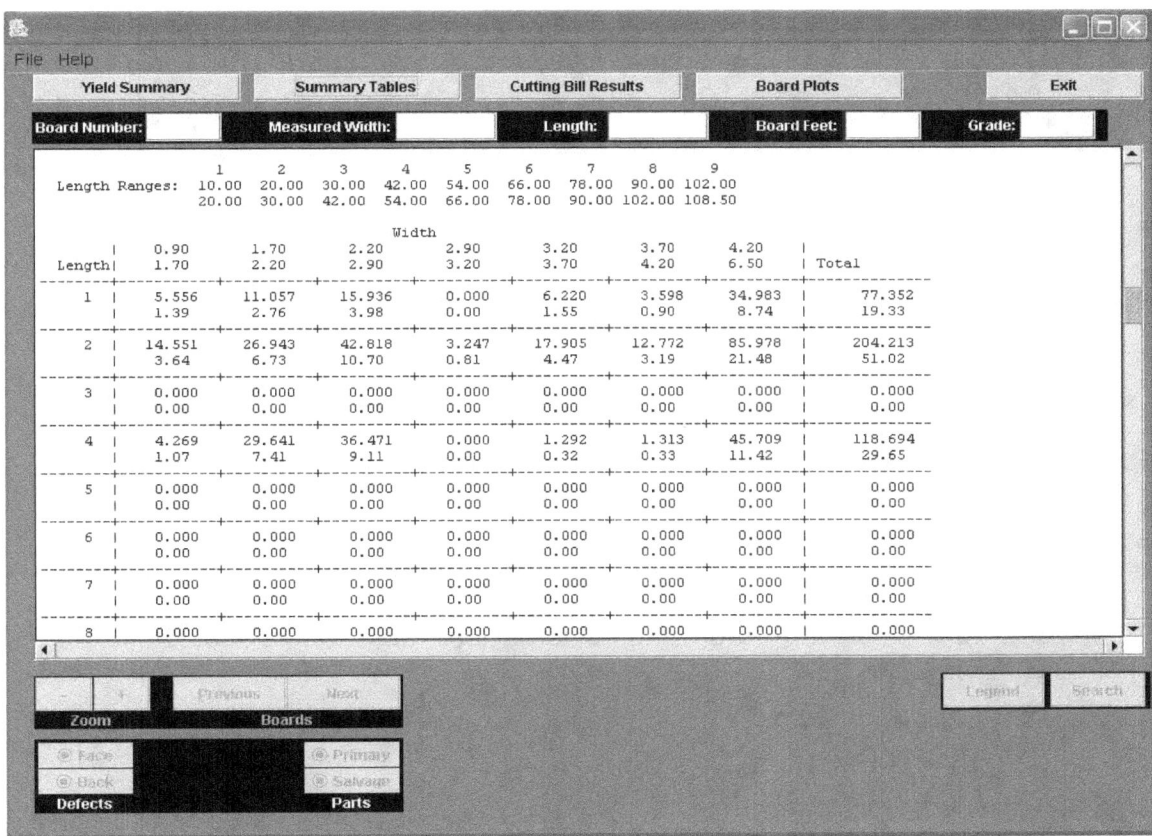

Figure 7.2a. Example Summary Table Results.

In each length-width cell, the upper number is the board feet of surface area and the lower number is the yield percentage. The percentages in all columns add to 100. The first table is the distribution of total yield. The second and third tables contain the surface-area distributions for the primary and salvage cuttings. The last three tables are based on the number of parts produced. These tables are organized in the same manner as the first three tables. In each length-width cell, the upper number is the part quantity and the lower number is the percentage of total part quantity.

7.3 Cutting Bill Results

The information generated by ROMI-3 when processing lumber to meet a cutting bill allows you to analyze the lumber volume, grade mix, and processing required to satisfy cutting bill requirements. Select *Cutting Bill Results* to view or print this type of information. As with summary tables, the first part of the cutting bill results contains processing and yield information. See Section 7.1 for a description of this output. A portion of the Cutting Bill Overall Part Quantity Obtained Report is shown in Figure 7.3a.

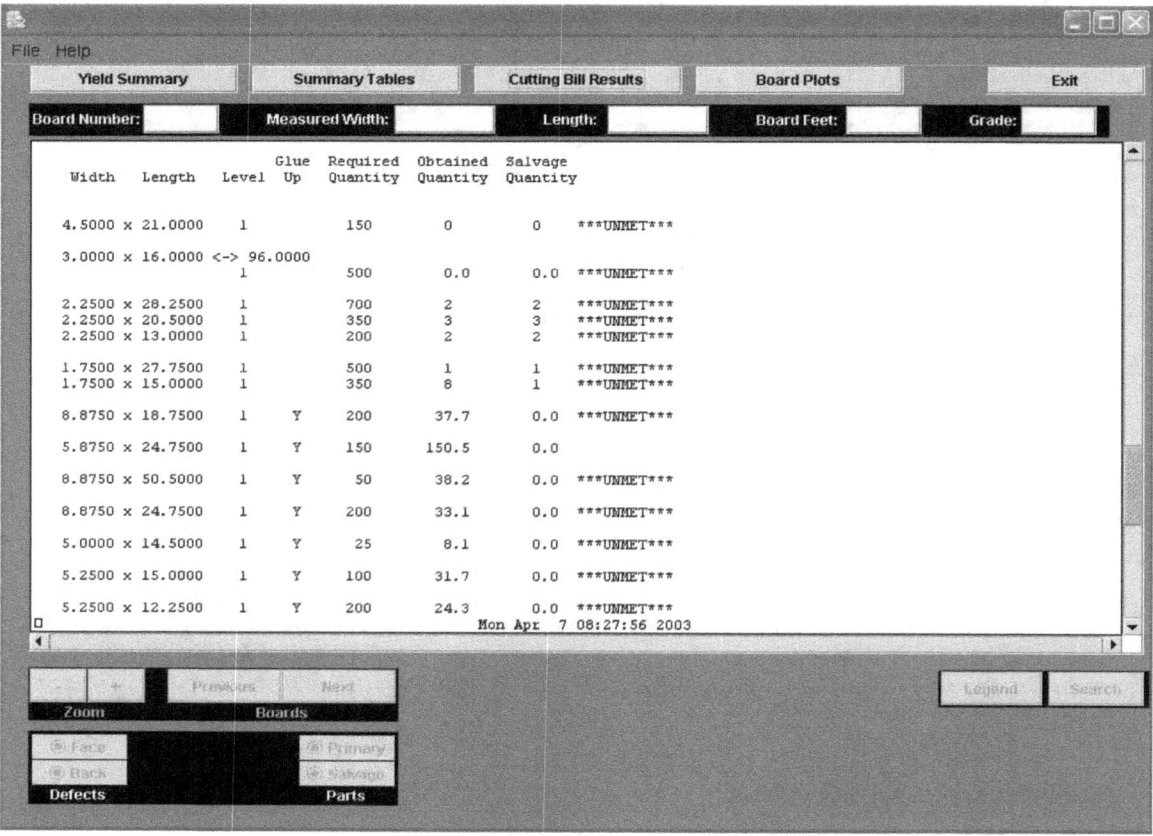

Figure 7.3a. Example Cutting Bill Results.

The width and length of each part is shown at left. For random-length parts, the minimum and maximum lengths are displayed to the right of the part's width on two lines. The Level column indicates the scheduling and replacement level number for that part.

7.4 Board Plots

ROMI-3 allows you to view or print plots of individual boards along with their parts, defects, and kerfs. The information used to generate board plots is maintained in output files with the extension .PLT. You can view board plots for an entire run or for a selected board by selecting *Board Plots* from the top of the viewer program. This brings up the board plot viewer window (Fig. 7.4a.).

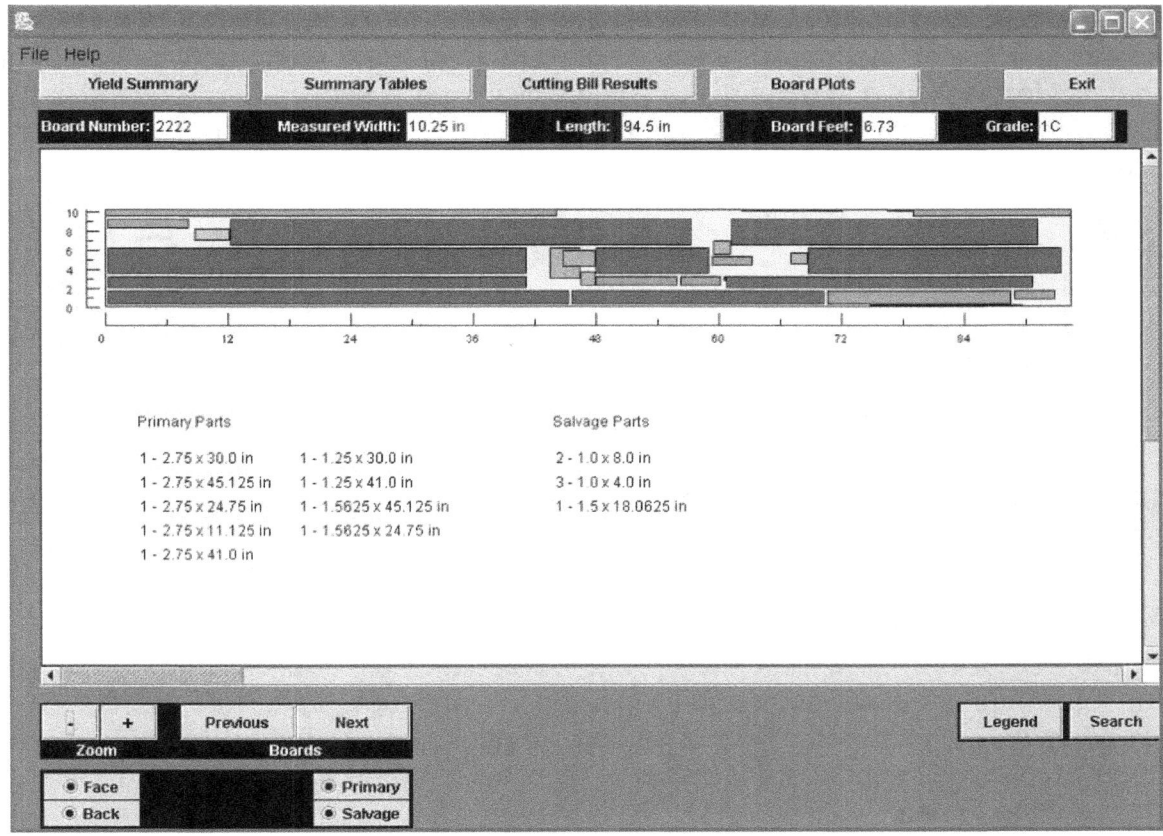

Figure 7.4a. Example Board Plots Results.

By default, it shows the first board in the file along with the first board processed. Click *Search* to choose a board for plotting by board number (Fig. 7.4b.).

Figure 7.4b. Example Board Search.

Boards are displayed as if they were transparent, with color-coded defects from both sides visible at once. The toggle buttons at the bottom of the screen are to turn on or off the defects for each side and the primary and salvage parts shown. Click *Legend* at the bottom of the screen for an explanation of the different defect colors (Fig. 7.4c.).

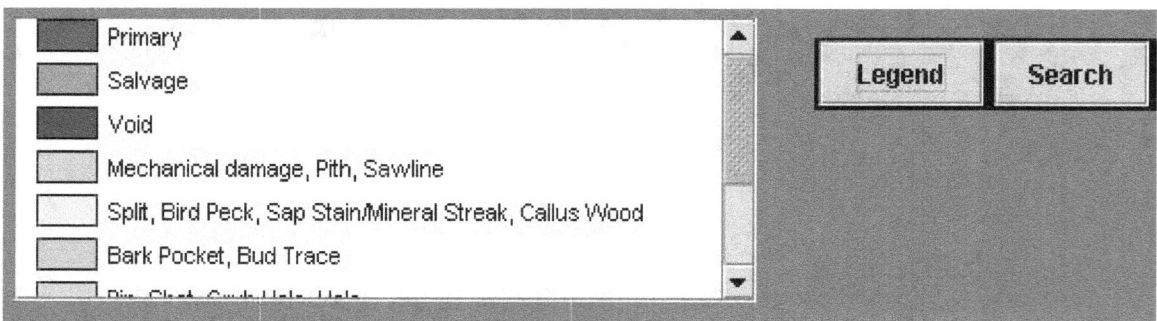
Figure 7.4c. Board Plot Legend.

Use the plus and minus zoom buttons to reduce or increase the size of the board in the viewer (Fig. 7.4a.). Click *Next* and *Previous* to see the next or previously viewed board. You can print the current board by clicking *File* and then *Print*. Note that the viewer prints only what is shown in the window. To print an entire board, you must zoom out so that the entire board is visible in the viewer. When you are finished, click *Exit* to close the viewer.

8. Least Cost Grade Mix

One of the most important features added to ROMI-3 is the least-cost grade mix calculator, which uses the methodology developed by Zou et al. (2004). This method is a significant departure from previous methods (Wodzinski et al.1966; Lawson et al.1996; Schumann et al.1971) that assumed a linear relationship between cutting bill yields and lumber grades. As shown by Zou et al., the existence of a linear relationship cannot always be guaranteed. ROMI-3 develops a series of yields that are based on the user's equipment settings, optimization settings, cutting bill demands, part grades, lumber costs, and processing costs. In this way, the least-cost solution is tailored exactly to the user's processing situation.

To use the least-cost grade mix module, you must be connected to the Internet as the least-cost program requires the use of the SAS (2002) statistics package. Rather than require each user to purchase SAS, we purchased a license that allows us to use a server for the analyses. This operates by ROMI-3 sending to the server your yield and cost data. The server analyzes the data and returns your least-cost grade mix solution. Anonymity is guaranteed because no identifying or other information is sent to the server, nor are any past results or data retained. It should be noted that users of ROMI-3 in some foreign countries may not be able to use the least-cost module due to the software license and technology used.

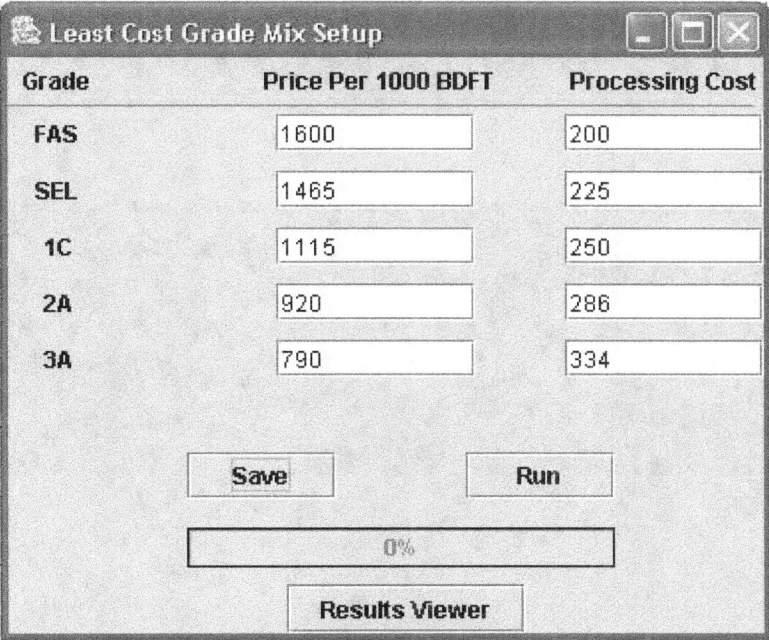

Figure 8.1a. Least Cost Grade Mix Setup.

8.1 Least Cost Grade Mix Setup

Clicking the Least Cost Grade Mix button in the main ROMI-3 interface (Fig. 2.4a) opens the window in Figure 8.1a.

Here the user can enter the cost of each board grade per 1,000 board feet as well as the cost to process 1,000 board feet of each grade. Clicking *Save* stores the information for later use. Clicking *Run* causes ROMI-3 to collect information from the current cutting bill and send it to the server for analysis. When the server is finished, the results are returned. The current window will close and the window in Figure 8.2a will open.

8.2 Least Cost Grade Mix Results

The Least Cost Grade Mix Results window (Figure 8.2a.) shows the cheapest cost grade mix. If a certain lumber grade is not desired in the results, click the check box next to the grade and the window will update with the next grade mix. The results of a least cost grade mix can be saved for future reference by clicking *Save Results* or clicking *File* and then *Save Results* (Figure 8.2b).

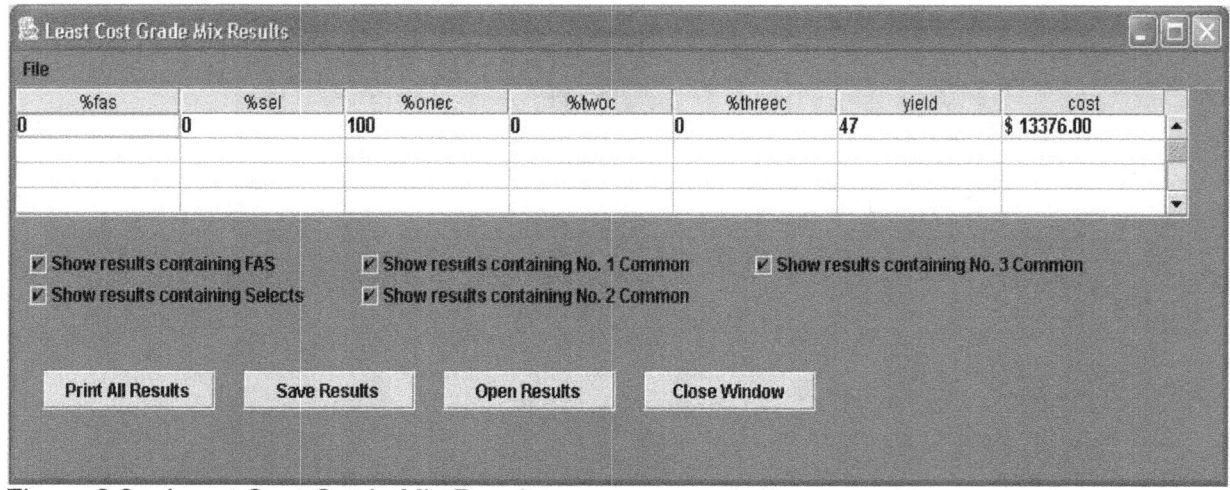

Figure 8.2a. Least Cost Grade Mix Results.

%fas	%sel	%onec	%twoc	%threec	yield	cost
0	0	100	0	0	47	$ 13376.00

☑ Show results containing FAS ☑ Show results containing No. 1 Common ☑ Show results containing No. 3 Common
☑ Show results containing Selects ☑ Show results containing No. 2 Common

Print All Results Save Results Open Results Close Window

Figure 8.2b. Least Cost Grade Mix Results Menu Options.

The saved results file will be saved with the .lcr file extension. If results are saved, the user can open the results viewer at any time by clicking *Open* and using the file chooser to open the results file. Clicking *Print All Results* or choosing it from the File menu opens a printer dialog that allows you to print all of the results. The results files may be large and require several pages to print. Close the Least Cost Grade Mix Results window by clicking *Close Window*.

9. The Mechanics of ROMI-3

Here we describe in detail how ROMI-3 processes lumber to match the demands of the cutting bill. Understanding the elements in this section will allow you to configure the ROMI-3 program to better simulate your rough-mill and processing conditions. The elements discussed in this section include gang-ripsaws, part prioritization, and salvage part processing.

9.1. Gang-Ripsaws

ROMI-3 simulates eight types of gang-ripsaws: 1) fixed arbor, 2) fixed arbor with movable outer blade, 3) fixed-blade-best-feed arbor, 4) simple fixed-blade-best-feed, 5) best-spacing-sequence, 6) best-spacing-sequence with movable-outer blade, 7) selective-rip arbor, and 8) an all-blades-movable arbor. Unless specified, all arbors process the board from the right edge to the left edge, with the right edge against the fence (Fig. 9.1). When simulating a fixed-arbor saw, the spacings are specified so that the first spacing is closest to the rip fence. The ripsaw kerf is adjustable to as narrow as 1/16 of an inch and as wide as 3/8 of an inch.

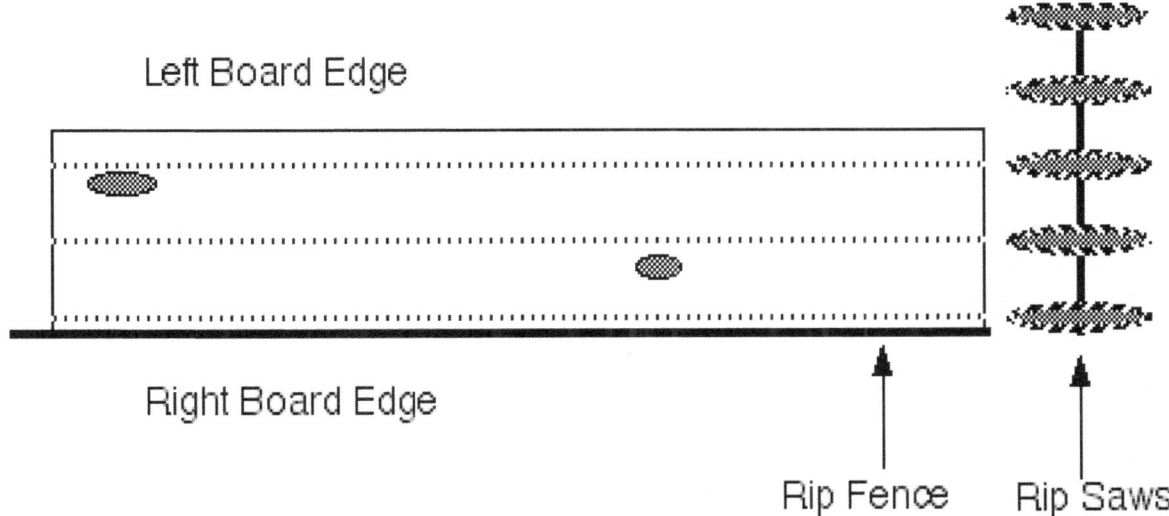

Figure 9.1. Rip-fence, board, and arbor relationship.

9.1.1. Fixed Blade Arbors

ROMI-3 has five fixed-blade arbor types: fixed, fixed with movable-outer blade, simple fixed-blade-best-feed, fixed-blade-best-feed, and selective rip. Fixed-blade-best-feed arbors simulate currently available optimizing lumber feeding systems. For all five fixed arbor configurations, the user specifies the saw spacing sequence by specifying as many as 15 spacings. Earlier versions of ROMI-RIP were limited with respect to the number of widths that could be placed on the arbor. ROMI-3 allows the user to include additional widths not included in the cutting bill that allow optimizing for the productions of widths for panels.

The fixed blade and fixed blade with movable outer blades are the simplest arbors available in ROMI-3. These arbors perform no optimization and rip every board with its right edge against the fence. This generates primary width strips and, in the case of the fixed-blade arbor, usually an edging strip. The moving-outer blade variant avoids generating narrow unusable edging strips. When using this arbor, ROMI-3 uses the minimum primary part width for making panels and uses that width in deciding when to move the outer saw blade. If the current spacings would generate an edging strip with less than the minimum acceptable primary width, the last blade is moved to the edge of the board and a single, wider, random-width strip is generated.

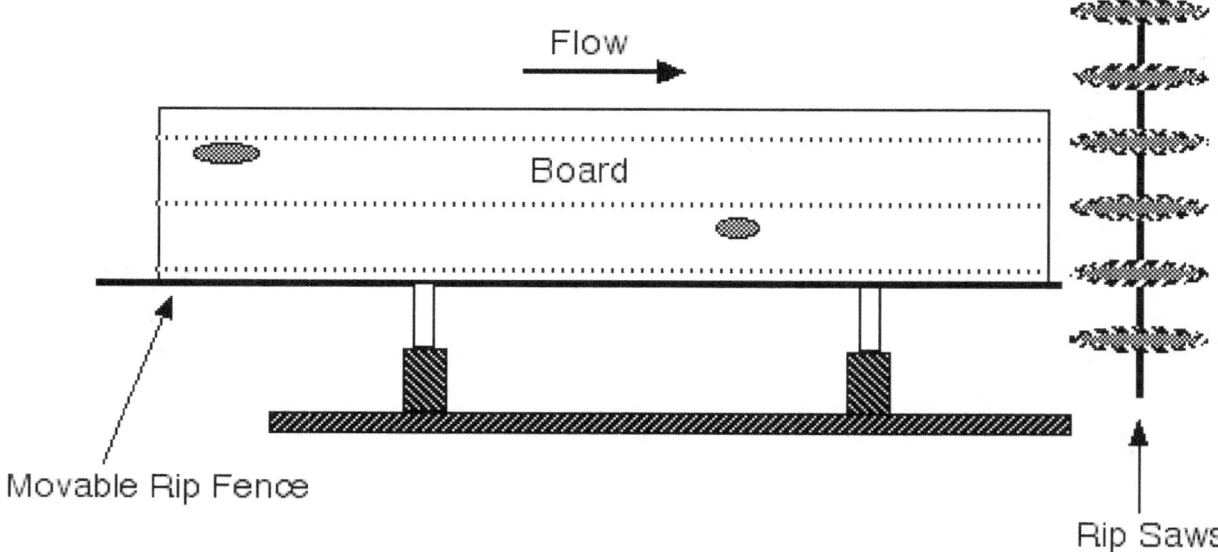

Figure 9.1.1. Fixed-blade-best-feed arbor layout.

The fixed-blade-best-feed arbors use a movable fence to optimize the placement of the board with respect to the saw blades on the arbor. Figure 9.1.1. shows the layout of the fixed-blade-best-feed arbors. The simple fixed-blade-best-feed arbor optimizes for the fitting of strip widths within each board with the goal of maximizing the accumulated width of the strips and minimizing the production of edgings. Although this is a valid optimization strategy that is used by many rough mills, the results of the optimization do not necessarily mean that the strips will reflect the demands of the cutting bill, or that the part yield from the strips will be satisfactory. The regular fixed-blade-best-feed arbor optimizes for the production of strips that will generate the highest prioritized value of parts as required by the cutting bill. In general, the simple fixed-blade-best-feed arbor obtains lower yields and requires more board footage to satisfy cutting bill requirements than the regular fixed-blade-best-feed arbor.

58

The selective-rip arbor models industrial selective-rip gang-ripsaws that are currently available. Like the other fixed-blade ripsaws, the user specifies the sequence of widths on the arbor. In addition, the user selects which saw blades are allowed to move on the arbor. There are two restrictions to the movement of saw blades: 1) movable saw blades cannot be adjacent, and 2) a movable saw blade can move no closer than 0.75 inch to another saw blade. The restriction in movement is due to the collars on the arbor that hold the saw blades. The selective rip arbor generally achieves the highest yield of any of the fixed-blade arbor variants. However, the higher yield comes at the cost of greater optimization and increased simulation processing time.

9.1.2. Best-Spacing-Sequence Arbors

The best-spacing-sequence arbors optimize the sequence of the saw spacings. The spacings are selected that will generate the greatest prioritized value of needed primary cuttings. See Section 9.2 for information on how part priorities are determined and how they affect the parts that are selected to be cut from each board.

The optimal placement of the saw spacings along an arbor is determined by an exhaustive search. Every possible combination of spacings is examined for each board. The actual number of spacings used is determined by an interaction between the board width and the specified cutting widths.

Earlier programs considered each possible combination of saw spacings separately. For example, consider the two spacing sequences: 2"-2"-1"-3" and 2"-2"-2"-3". RIPYLD and its successors would determine the yield from the first set of saw spacings and then determine the yield for the second set. The yield from the first two spacings (2"-2") would be determined twice. However, yields from the first two spacings need to be determined only once for any given board as the yield from the 2"-2" spacings will be the same. ROMI-3 uses a recursive function to construct a series of possible strip sequences. The recursive function tracks the yield and strip sequence up to the current strip. Because each possible strip is examined only once, processing time is reduced dramatically.

The best-spacing-sequence arbor with movable-outer blade operates much like the best-spacing-sequence arbor discussed previously. A movable-outer blade is added to eliminate any edging. This arbor assumes that random pieces are acceptable. An additional strip width, narrower than all the primary widths, is specified (see Section 3.2.6) and represents the minimum width acceptable for gluing up into panels. After ROMI-3 determines the best-spacing sequence, the remainder of the board is examined. If the remainder meets or exceeds the additional narrow strip width, the processing continues. If it is narrower, the last specified width is not taken. Then the last saw blade is moved to the outer edge of the board and a wider random-width strip is sawn.

9.1.3. All-Blades-Movable Arbor

The all-blades-movable arbor is unique among arbors with at least one fixed-saw spacing. Because there is no preset width, the saw spacings usually are set by the amount of the highest priority cuttings that can be obtained. These usually are the widest and longest cuttings. In addition, a new "null" saw spacing is added to enable the saw to box in defects into narrow waste strips at any point on the board face. For example, a board containing a large amount of pith and associated small knots along the middle of the board could use a null strip to box in the defects. The inclusion of null strips usually results in wider strips with fewer defects. Null widths from 3/4 to 2-1/2 inches can be generated depending on the maximum yield of primary cuttings and board characteristics.

Simulating the all-blades-movable arbor is similar to the best-spacing-sequence arbors discussed earlier. The only difference is that spacer widths are added to the primary widths to allow for the creation of the null spacings. Spacer widths determine the possible random width distances between the fixed-width primary strips. Three spacer widths, 3/4, 1, and 1-1/4 inch, are used to simulate all possible random-width null spacings greater than 3/4 inch. To limit the number of combinations that must be examined, the maximum null spacing is 2-1/2 inches and the minimum spacing between saws is 3/4 inch. The latter spacing is based on the fact that most currently available selective-rip gang-ripsaws with movable-blade arbors can move saws no closer than 3/4 inch.

9.1.4. Optimizing Arbor Comparison

Each of the five optimizing arbors (best-spacing-sequence, fixed-blade-best-feed, simple fixed-blade-best-feed, selective-rip, and all-blades-movable) have different optimizing characteristics and give different yields. For comparison, a 2A Common board (#3159 measuring 9" x 96.5 with 6 board feet) was sawn using the different arbors. Figure 9.1.4 shows the different gang-rip solutions for board 3159 given the different arbor types. Table 1 shows the cutting bill used for these examples. The CDE prioritization strategy was used to prioritize parts during processing. Table 2 summarizes the volumes of parts and percent yields obtained from the sample board for each optimizing arbor. Figure 9.1.4 shows the rip and chop solution for each of the optimizing arbors.

Table 1.--Cutting bill used to process sample board 3159 shown in Figure 9.1.4

Width	Length	Quantity
Inches	*Inches*	*Number*
4	58	200
4	18	400
4	14	100
4	8	50
2.75	52	200
2.75	41.5	150
2.75	34	100
2.75	22	125
2.75	20	150
2.75	18	50
2.75	14	150
2.75	8	100
12 panel	24	50
10 panel	20	50

Table 2.--Optimizing arbor part volume and yield comparison for 2AC board 3159

Arbor type	Primary		Salvage		Total	
	Part volume	Percent yield	Part volume	Percent yield	Part volume	Percent yield
	Board feet		*Board feet*		*Board feet*	
Best-spacing-sequence	3.65	60.83	0.23	3.83	3.88	64.67
Fixed-blade-best-feed	4.11	68.50	0.00	0.00	4.11	68.50
Simple fixed-blade-best-feed	4.22	70.33	0.00	0.00	4.22	70.33
Selective-rip	3.97	66.17	0.23	3.83	4.20	70.00
All-blades-movable	3.97	66.17	0.23	3.83	4.20	70.00

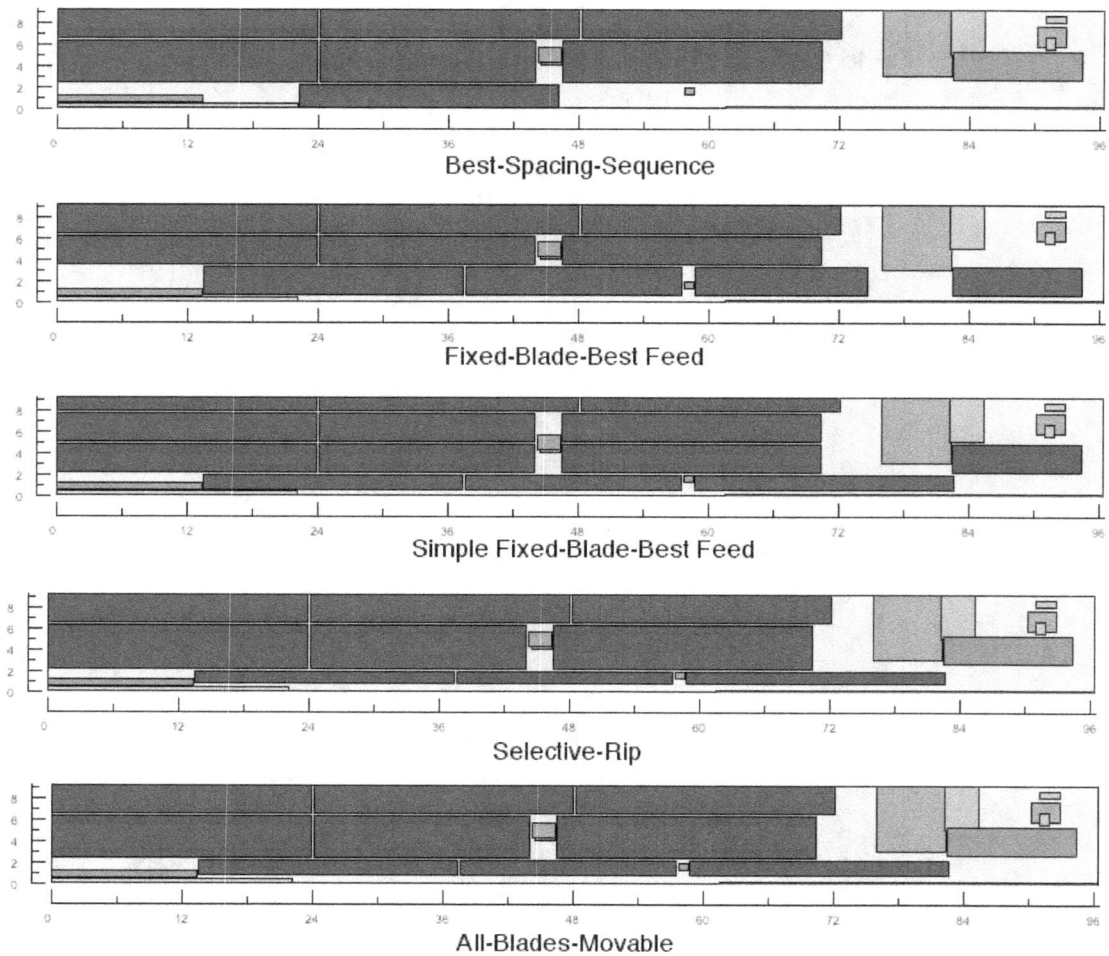

Figure 9.1.4. Sample board sawn using, from top, the best-spacing-sequence, fixed-blade-best-feed, simple fixed-blade-best-feed, selective-rip, and all-blades-movable arbors.

The best-spacing-sequence arbor obtained the lowest yield of the optimizing arbors examined. However, like the movable-blade arbors, the best-spacing-sequence arbor was able to obtain the wider (4.0 inch) parts. As these size parts can be difficult to obtain using 2A Common, this solution still is desirable.

The simple fixed-blade-best-feed (SFBBF) arbor had the highest yield followed by the fixed-blade-best-feed (FBBF) arbor. The simulated hardware of these two arbors are identical except in how the cutting solution is optimized. Although SFBBF obtained a higher yield, it does not consider cutting bill requirements when it makes its optimization decision, that is, it considers only optimizing the accumulated width of cuttings within the board. Therefore, toward the end of processing when some widths are no longer required, it may be difficult to obtain strip widths with part needs using SFBBF.

The selective-rip (SR) arbor starts with the optimal spacing arrangement used by FBBF and SFBBF, but is allowed to move user-specified spacings to obtain difficult-to-obtain part sizes and to maximize yield and cutting opportunities. The all-blades-movable (ABM) arbor simply moves all blades and has the same advantages of the SR but with greater flexibility. Both SR and ABM had the third highest yield among the optimizing arbors. The solutions from the two arbors are identical for this board due to similarities in the simulated hardware and optimizing methods. The solutions from SR and ABM returned wider, more valuable, and difficult-to-obtain parts than FBBF and SFBBF.

9.1.5. How to Optimize Fixed-Blade Saw Spacing Sequences

Charles Gatchell (1996), an expert in rough mill systems and optimization, stated: "There are thousands of ways to arrange a few different saw spacings. Most are poor and unrealistic...." He added that successfully optimizing the sequence of fixed-blade saw spacings requires that the user know the width distribution of the lumber to be processed and the volume of finished parts required in each part width, and that the user needs to recognize that an arbor is not just a sequence of spacings but a sequence of combinations that overlap and interact. Gatchell's publication, "Designing a Fixed-Blade Gang Ripsaw Arbor with a Pencil," does an excellent job of showing how to easily design arbors that are near optimal (if not optimal).

The fixed-blade arbor optimization tool included with ROMI-3 automates the method designed by Gatchell. ROMI-3 makes a single optimization run with the user-specified cutting bill and lumber data using the best-spacing-sequence arbor. Recall that this arbor generates for each board the optimal fixed-blade saw spacing sequence. As ROMI-3 processes boards, it remembers the set of saw spacing sequences. The sequences not only show the optimal solution for each board but represent the interaction between board widths and cutting bill width requirements. For example, part widths with higher requirements are used more often and appear more often in the set of sequences.

ROMI-3 sorts and summarizes the set of saw spacing sequences and begins building the arbor with the sequence that is used most often. The optimizer adds sequences to the arbor such that the interaction between the spacings provides the most optimal combination and does not repeat an existing combination. See Section 3.2.5 on how to run the ROMI-3 arbor optimizer.

9.2. Part Prioritization

Interactions among length, width, and quality of boards and parts are critical for efficient processing. The goal is to cut only needed parts from as little lumber as possible while minimizing the production of "orphan" parts. Longer and wider parts are much more difficult to obtain from the lower grades. Lumber quality varies from board to board within a lumber grade. As a result, a method is needed to prioritize the parts so that the simulator can decide which part size to cut.

ROMI-3 allows the user to select one of several part prioritizing strategies based on area, or dollar value, or automatically assigned parts values using one of the programs dynamic strategies. The goal of these strategies is to meet all of a cutting bill's required cuttings using the least amount of lumber. Value- and area-based strategies are included because they are historical and might better simulate a user's rough mill. Although these methods are static in nature (the first and last pieces cut for a part size have the same priority), we have included a simple modifier for each that make them somewhat dynamic. However, the recommended strategy is the dynamic exponent method.

9.2.1. Value-Based Part Prioritizing

ROMI-3 contains two value-based part prioritization strategies: PART VALUE and DYNAMIC PART VALUE. PART VALUE is similar to strategies used in earlier rough-mill simulations such as CORY (Brunner 1987). With part valuing, each part size is assigned a value. The decision on which parts are needed more are given a higher value. Smaller part sizes are given a lower value. Obviously, results can differ when different part values are used. In reality, the values assigned to the different part sizes may or may not reflect the actual value of the part. The simulation is highly dependent on the user's assumptions about the values.

Most dollar-valuation systems cannot consider needed part quantities. If a part is valued high at the beginning of processing, it will have the same high value at the end of processing even if the required number of cuttings are met shortly after processing begins. A better solution is to reduce the value of the part as its requirements are met (DYNAMIC PART VALUE). This shifts the emphasis from quantity requirements for parts that are nearly satisfied to those that are not being met. If the required quantity for a part size is N, the value of the part is reduced $1/N$ each time a part is cut. For example, if you value a part size at $1.00 and require 50 of them, cutting one part of this size will reduce the value of the next part to $0.98.

9.2.2. Area-Based Part Prioritizing

ROMI-3 contains three part prioritization strategies based on part area: AREA, L^2W, and L^2W x NEED. AREA part prioritization equally prioritizes the width and length of parts and is the true yield optimization prioritization mode, so the highest overall yield can be expected when using this method. However, because AREA places no emphasis on wider or longer parts, it is likely to prioritize parts inconsistent with the demands of the cutting bill. The L^2W strategy is the same formula found in the YIELD program developed by Thomas (1962), CORY (Brunner et al. 1987), and the Forest Products Laboratory's YIELD program (Wodzinski and Hahm 1966). L^2W builds in a preference for longer cuttings and is more likely to correspond to cutting bill requirements. However, it does not consider part quantity.

Cutting bills in which the numbers of different parts vary greatly are difficult to analyze. A simple improvement to the L²W formula is L²W x NEED (Thomas 1996). L²W multiplied by NEED, the current number of parts required for a particular part size, results in a L²W strategy that is sensitive to quantity demands. Overall performance is improved. As a part is cut, the need for that part size is decreased by one. The L²W x NEED strategy can be regarded as a simple dynamic strategy.

9.2.3 Dynamic Part Prioritizing

Dynamic part prioritizing strategies seek to overcome many of the problems associated with dollar- or area-based strategies. Dynamic strategies are distinguished from others by the ability to reduce priorities as part requirements are met. Rather than depend on part size alone or on an operator's judgment as to which values to assign to different part sizes, dynamic strategies assign each part size a priority based on its size and needed quantity. This allows cutting preference to shift from parts with quantities that are nearly met to those that require a greater quantity.

ROMI-3's dynamic strategies calculate exponential weighting factors based on the needed quantity of a part size. The value of these exponential factors typically ranges from 1.0 to 3.2 depending on the needed quantity of the part size. ROMI-3 allows the user to choose from two exponential part prioritizing strategies: Simple Dynamic Exponent (SDE) or Complex Dynamic Exponent (CDE). As the name implies, CDE considers more information about the cutting bill's current requirements than SDE when assigning part priorities. For example, CDE is sensitive not only to how many parts are currently needed for each size but also to how many have been cut. This is useful when a cutting bill contains large parts with relatively small needed quantities. Obviously, large parts will be harder to obtain. With only a quantity-based exponential weighting factor, these parts may not receive high enough priority to be obtained opportunistically. CDE increases the priority of such parts so that they can be obtained at earlier and/or more opportune times in processing.

CDE and SDE should not be confused with dynamic variants of the value- and area-based strategies. The simplistic dynamic value and area strategies mentioned earlier reduce their priorities linearly; CDE and SDE reductions are exponential. A major drawback to linear reductions is that the priority of a part is reduced much more rapidly than with the exponential method (Fig. 9.2.3.). The key advantage of the CDE and SDE strategies is that they maintain priority levels until most of the required cuttings for the part have been obtained. Figure 9.2.3 shows a comparison between the linear dynamic area strategy and the exponential CDE strategy. A full discussion of the evolution of the dynamic prioritizing strategies is found in "Prioritizing Parts From Cutting Bills When Gang Ripping First" (Thomas 1996).

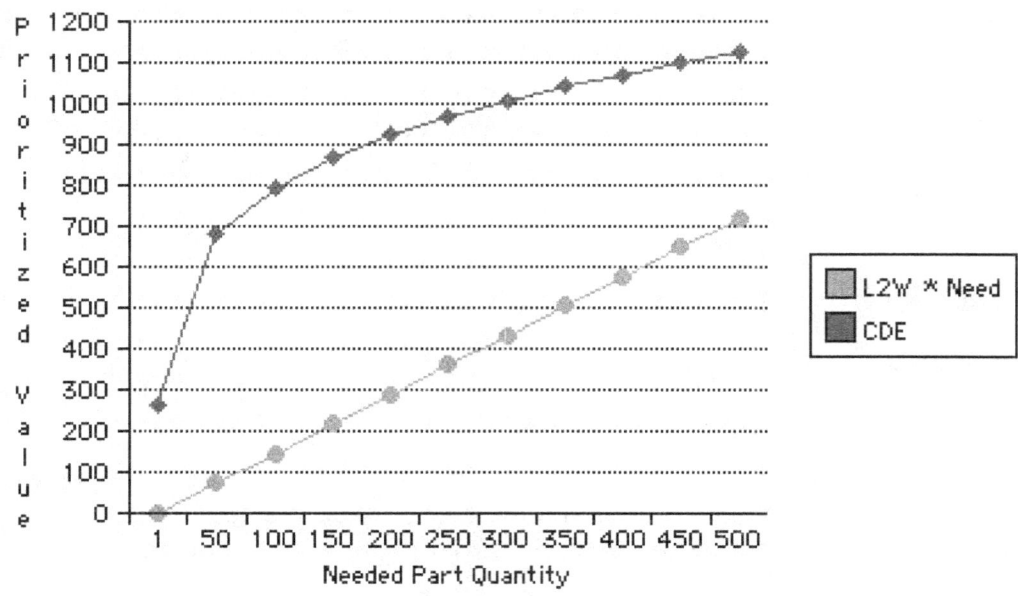

Figure 9.2.3. L²W x Need and CDE prioritizing comparison for a 2- by 48-inch part.

9.2.4 Selecting a Part-Prioritizing Strategy

ROMI-3's default part prioritizing strategy is CDE. CDE usually prioritizes parts so they can be obtained from the least amount of lumber. However, this level of efficiency may be too high for some users. If chopsaws are being run on a longest-length-first basis, the L²W or L²W x Need strategies might predict yield better. Or if a system requires a part valuing approach, ROMI-RIP's value-based strategies might be useful.

9.3. Processing Salvage Parts

Clear areas of a strip section that do not contain primary parts but can contain salvage parts are called salvage areas. Finding salvage areas requires a more complex search procedure than that used for finding clear primary area. ROMI-3 performs three distinct steps during salvage operations: 1) locate all clear salvage areas, 2) determine which area to work on first, and 3) cut out the salvage part(s). The remainder of this section describes these steps.

9.3.1. Locating Clear Salvage Areas

To find clear salvage areas, each strip section that remains after primary parts are removed is examined using a modified corkscrew method. From a starting point, a corkscrew is generated that moves outward in a counter clockwise direction. The corkscrew expands 1/2 inch in length for every 1/4 inch in width. The corkscrew is

66

expanded until an edge meets a cutting, defect, or strip edge. When this occurs to any edge, the remaining edges continue to be expanded until all edges have contacted a cutting, defect, or strip edge. Ultimately, a clear rectangular salvage area is described by the edges of the corkscrew.

9.3.2. Selecting a Clear Area

Long, thin salvage usually is not wanted. To increase the preference for wider salvage cuttings, an exponential weighting factor is applied to the width of the clear areas. The formula for determining the weighting area for a clear area is:

$$Weighted\ Area = Length\ x\ Width^{Weighting\ Factor}$$

The weighted areas are then compared with one another. The weighting factor will cause a preference for a slightly wider and shorter area over a narrower and longer area even if the longer, narrower section has greater area. However, ROMI-3 will take longer, narrower areas that are at least 10 to 15 percent larger than shorter, wider areas.

In general, the preference for shorter, wider areas comes at the cost of longer, narrower cuttings and requires more crosscuts. As the weighting factor increases, so does the preference for shorter, wider cuttings. ROMI-3 actually cuts parts that fill in the spaces between defects and other cuttings.

Several comparisons of different salvage-area weighting factors with different part sizes showed that the greatest increase in yield occurs when the weighting factor is less than 1.9. There was little difference in yield or part sizes when the weighting factor was between 1.6 and 2.1. If the weighting factor was increased significantly (above 2.5), yield sometimes decreased while the number of salvage parts increased! The salvage width weighting preference for ROMI-3 is set at 1.9. The number of rips required actually decrease slightly as the wider salvage parts often are located on one edge of the strip.

9.3.3. Producing the Salvage Part

When the available clear area for a salvage part is identified, several options are available to determine which part size to cut from the clear area. The simplest option takes the full width of the area to generate a random-width part. For this method, the user needs to specify the minimum acceptable salvage width. A second method rips the area to the widest possible specified primary-part width. The third method rips the area to the widest possible salvage-part width. Salvage-part widths are specified by the user separately from the primary widths and are used only for salvage.

Three methods can be used to determine which salvage-part length to cut. The simplest method takes the longest random length possible with respect to the minimum and maximum primary-part lengths. The second method takes the longest primary-part length that will fit. A third method takes the longest salvage-part length. Salvage specific part lengths are specified separately from the primary lengths.

After the first salvage part has been cut, the remaining area is examined. Cuttings are removed until there is no area large enough for the smallest salvage cutting.

9.3.4. Smart Salvage

If specified, ROMI-3 attempts to cut a part from salvage that is needed by the cutting bill (Section 3.2.7). ROMI-3 first determines the widest possible primary part that will fit in the clear salvage area. Then a check is made to see that there is a need for part lengths that will fit in the clear area. If any are needed, the most desirable (depending on part-prioritization strategy) primary-size part is cut. If there is no need for that size, the largest primary part that fits the clear area is cut.

The benefits of salvaging according to the cutting bill are maximized when primary operations are prevented from cutting orphan or excess parts. This allows the salvage operations to look at larger areas and potentially cut larger parts that are needed by the cutting bill. This approximates the re-saw or re-rip operations found in rough mills and other simulators. Re-saw involves re-ripping a strip to a width that will yield a part needed by the cutting bill. This operation is called "smart salvage."

Figure 9.3a shows a strip where all possible primary parts have been cut from the full-width clear area and one salvage part from the right end. In this example, only the left-most parts are needed by the cutting bill. The remaining primary part is an excess or orphan part. Figure 9.3b shows the same strip processed when the primary operations cut only needed parts. This yielded two needed parts and one needed primary-size salvage part.

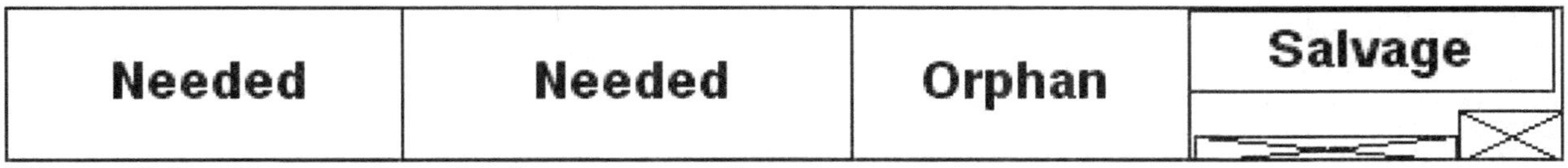

Needed	Needed	Orphan	Salvage

Figure 9.3a. Conventional primary operation.

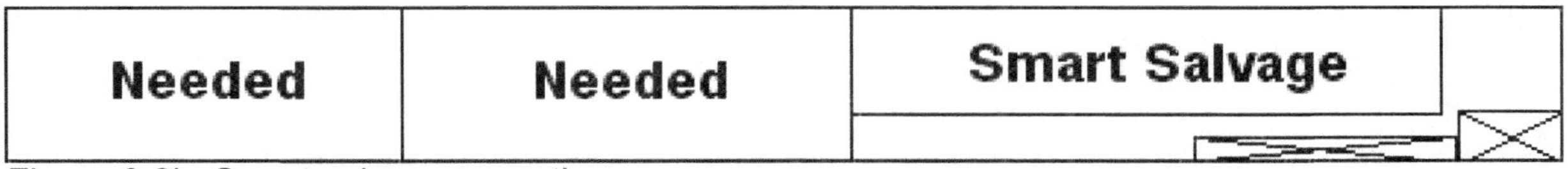

Needed	Needed	Smart Salvage	

Figure 9.3b. Smart salvage operation.

Although smart salvage reduces salvage yield, it can reduce the amount of lumber required to meet a cutting bill. ROMI-3 simulations, comparing yields between smart salvage and standard operations across several cutting bills and lumber grades, show a reduction of 0.4 to 2.2 percent in the total amount of lumber required. There are several factors that can influence this reduction. Obviously, if the cutting bill is well matched to the lumber, there are few orphans, and the yield is acceptable, the benefits from using smart salvage will be lower. Sawing wider strips increases smart-salvage chances of finding required cuttings.

Literature Cited

Brunner, C.C.; White, M.S.; Lamb, F.M.; Schroeder, J.G. 1987. **CORY: a computer program for determining dimension stock yields.** Forest Products Journal. 39(2): 23-24.

Gatchell, Charles J. 1996. **Designing a fixed-blade gang ripsaw arbor with a pencil.** Forest Products Journal. 46(6): 37-40.

Gatchell, Charles J.; Thomas, R. Edward; Walker, Elizabeth S. 1998. **1998 data bank for kiln-dried red oak lumber.** Gen. Tech. Rep. NE-245. Radnor, PA: U.S. Department of Agriculture, Forest Service, Northeastern Research Station. 47 p.

Lawson, Penny; Thomas, R. Edward; Walker, Elizabeth. 1996. **OPTIGRAMI: Optimum V2 user's guide.** Gen. Tech. Rep. NE-190. Radnor. PA: U.S. Department of Agriculture, Forest Service, Northeastern Forest Experiment Station. 46 p.

Moody, John; Gatchell, Charles J.; Walker, Elizabeth S.; Klinkhachorn, Powsiri. 1998. **User's guide to UGRS: the Ultimate Grading and Remanufacturing System (version 5.0).** Gen. Tech. Rep. NE-254. Radnor, PA: U.S. Department of Agriculture, Forest Service, Northeastern Research Station. 40 p.

National Hardwood Lumber Association. 1998. **Rules for the measurement and inspection of hardwood and cypress lumber.** Memphis, TN: National Hardwood Lumber Association.

SAS Institute. 2002. **SAS system for windows 8.2.** Cary, NC: SAS Institute.

Schumann, D.R. 1971. **Dimension yields from black walnut lumber.** Res. Pap. FPL-162. Madison, WI: U.S. Department of Agriculture, Forest Service, Forest Products Laboratory. 16 p.

Stiess, Timothy S. 1995. **Simulation in the wood products industry.** Wood & Wood Products. September: 133-135.

Thomas, R. Edward. 1996. **Prioritizing parts from cutting bills when gang-ripping first.** Forest Products Journal. 46(10): 61-66.

Thomas, R. Edward. 1997. **ROMI-CROSS: ROugh MILL CROSScut-first simulator.** Gen. Tech. Rep. NE-229. Radnor, PA: U.S. Department of Agriculture, Forest Service, Northeastern Forest Experiment Station. 56 p.

Thomas, R. Edward. 1999. **User's Guide to ROMI-RIP 2.0: A ROugh MILL RIP-first simulator.** Gen. Tech. Rep. NE-259. Radnor, PA: U.S. Department of Agriculture, Forest Service, Northeastern Research Station. 64 p.

Thomas, Richard J. 1962. **The rough end yield research program.** Forest Products Journal. 12(11): 536-537.

Wodzinski, C.; Hahm, E. 1966. **A computer program to determine yields of lumber.** Gen. Tech. Rep. FPJ-66-009. Madison, WI: U.S. Department of Agriculture, Forest Service, Forest Products Laboratory. 34 p.

Zou, Xiaoqui; Buehlmann, Urs; Thomas, R. Edward. 2004. **Investigating the linearity assumptuion between lumber grade mix and yield using design of experiments (DOE).** Wood and Fiber Science. 36(4): 547-559.

Appendix I. System Limitations

These are the current specifications and limitations of the ROMI-3 simulator:

Board width:	48 inches (1.219 meters)
Board length:	Unlimited
Cutting bill	
Maximum individual part quantity:	32,000
Maximum individual part value:	32,000
Maximum number of part sizes:	400
Board data files processed at once:	10
Length ranges:	10
Width ranges:	15
Lengths	
Primary:	30 or random
Salvage:	15 or random
Widths	
Primary:	20 or random
Salvage:	15 or random
Gang ripsaw arbor	
Width:	48
Number of Spacings:	15

Appendix II. Board Data Bank Description

The contents of the individual datafiles included with ROMI-3 are described. All datafiles have an eight-letter primary file name followed by a .DAT extension. All of the boards in each datafile are one of six grades. The grade of lumber in a particular datafile is determined by looking at the file name.

File Name	Grade
FAS	FAS (formerly Firsts and Seconds)
F1F	FAS One Face
SEL	Selects
1C	No. 1 Common
2AC	No. 2A Common
3AC	No. 3A Common

The boards supplied with ROMI-3 are found in "1998 Data Bank for Kiln-Dried Red Oak Lumber" (Gatchell et al. 1998). The following tables show the total number of boards in each of the six grades. The boards in each grade are sorted randomly into subsets containing approximately the same number of boards. Datafiles ending with a letter contain boards that are mirror images of their corresponding files with number endings. For example, 1C-A contains boards that are mirror images of the boards in 1C-1, 2AC-3 mirrors boards in 2AC-3, and so on. MIX files contain all boards, both normal and mirrored, for the grade.

Lumber grade	No. of boards	Board footage	Number of subsets
FAS	659	5,134	10
F1F	348	2,552	5
Selects	279	1,052	2
No. 1 Common	1,039	5,887	11
No. 2A Common	922	4,737	9
No. 3A Common	240	1,012	2

Appendix III. Definition of Terms

All-Blades-Movable Arbor: An arbor on which all blades are allowed to move to generate specified or random-width strips that best match the characteristics of the board and the demands of the cutting bill.

Best-Spacing-Sequence Arbor: The best fixed blade saw spacing arrangement is generated for each board starting one edge against the rip fence.

Board Segment: A full-width section of a board produced by crosscutting the board to a part length. Board segments are ripped to produce one or more primary parts.

Cutting Bill: A specified list of part sizes and quantities. For ROMI-CROSS, the cutting bill may include part prioritization methods based on dollar values or other methods. See also: Dynamic Prioritization Methods and Static Prioritization Methods.

Cutting Stage: A single ripping or crosscut operation. Crosscutting a board into primary part length board sections is a single cutting stage. The production of primary parts requires two stages: crosscutting and ripping.

Dynamic Prioritization Method: A method of prioritizing parts required in a cutting bill so that the part priorities change as parts are produced. Dynamic methods generally require less board footage than static methods to meet a given cutting bill. See also *Cutting Bill and Static Prioritization Methods*.

Excess Part: See **Orphan Part**.

Excess Primary Part: Part produced in two cutting stages for which there is no requirement in the cutting bill, but whose width and length, in combination are found in the cutting bill.

Excess Salvage Part: Part produced in three or more cutting stages for which there is no requirement in the cutting bill. The first stage is always the initial crosscut.

Fixed Arbor: The saw spacing arrangement specified by the user and used for all boards. Each board is ripped with one edge against the left edge of the arbor.

Fixed-Blade-Best-Feed Arbor: The saw spacing arrangement specified by the user and used for all boards. Each board is positioned automatically with respect to the saw spacings such that the strips generated best match the characteristics of the board and the demands of the cutting bill.

Kerf: The amount of wood removed by a saw blade. Common kerf thickness simulated by ROMI-3 are 0.125 and 0.1875 inch.

Minimum Primary Width: The minimum primary width that is specified when processing random width part sizes.

Movable-Outer-Blade: An arbor on which the last blade can be moved out to the edge of the board. The blade is moved out if an edging strip less than the minimum primary width would be generated. This produces a single, wider random-width strip.

Orphan Part: A primary part that is cut but is not needed; that is, the cutting needs for a particular part size have been met already. An "extra" piece.

Panel: A panel is made up of two or more edge-glued pieces of specified length and width.

Primary: Parts produced by ripping board sections to primary part widths.

Primary Part Widths: The part widths used when ripping board segments to specified part sizes. Any part width listed in a cutting bill is a primary part width.

Primary Part Lengths: Any length specified in a cutting bill is specified as a primary part length. The primary part lengths are the lengths that are crosscut from the board.

Salvage: Parts that are obtained by at least one additional cutting operation. The additional work makes these parts more expensive to produce and, therefore, less desirable. Unlike excess salvage, salvage parts are required by the cutting bill.

Saw Spacing Sequence: The sequence or arrangement of widths on the arbor. It is important that this sequence be developed in consideration of the width distribution of the lumber and the surface area required for each part width. For additional information see (Gatchell 1996).

Selective-Rip Arbor: The saw spacing arrangement is specified by the user and is used for all boards. The user specifies which blades are fixed and which are movable. For movable blades, the distance they are allowed to move also must be sequence such that the strips generated best match the characteristics of the board and the demands of the cutting bill.

Static Prioritization Method: A method of prioritizing cutting bill parts. The priority assigned to a cutting bill part at the start of processing is the same priority used at the end of processing. Number or dollar values are good examples of a static prioritization strategy. Static prioritization generally is less efficient than dynamic strategies. See also **Cutting Bill and Dynamic Prioritization Methods.**

Strip: A narrow, board-length piece of wood produced by the gang ripsaw.

Weiss, Joel M.; Thomas, R. Edward, 2004. **ROMI-3: Rough-Mill Simulator Version 3.0: User's Guide**. Gen. Tech. Rep. NE-328. Newtown Square, PA: U.S. Department of Agriculture, Forest Service, Northeastern Research Station. 75 p.

ROMI-3 Rough-Mill Simulator is a software package that simulates current industrial practices for rip-first and chop-first lumber processing. This guide shows the user how to set up and examine the results of simulations of current or proposed mill practices. ROMI-3 accepts cutting bills with as many as 600 combined solid and/or panel part sizes. Plots of processed boards are easily viewed or printed, as are detailed summaries of processing data (number of rips and crosscuts) and yields for each grade.

Keywords: gang-rip-first; chop-first; lumber processing; secondary processing; computer simulation